MANAGING TRADE DISPUTES EFFECTIVELY FOR A BETTER INDUSTRIAL RELATION

MANAGING TRADE DISPUTES EFFECTIVELY FOR A BETTER INDUSTRIAL RELATION

AN INSIGHT TO MORE THAN 30 REAL LIFE CASES
SUCH ASUNION RECOGNITION, UNION MANAGEMENT,
COLLECTIVE BARGAINING, DISMISSAL, VSS,
AND RETRENCHMENT SCHEME AND OTHERS

ABDUL RAHMAN @MARIDAN RAMLI

PARTRIDGE
A Penguin Random House Company

To order additional copies of this book, contact
Toll Free 800 101 2657 (Singapore)
Toll Free 1 800 81 7340 (Malaysia)
orders.singapore@partridgepublishing.com

www.partridgepublishing.com/singapore

CONTENTS

DEDICATED TO THE ever LOVING MEMORY
OF MY LATE SON, KHALIQ ZAMIR WHO
PASSED AWAY PEACEFULLY IN 2010

ACKNOWLEDGMENTS

I would like to express my deepest and sincerest gratitude to the following persons; Mr Alfred Charles, a senior HR consultant and a book author on "A-Z Guide to Employment Practice in Malaysia" published by CCH Asia Pte Limited. He was responsible in giving me the encouragement to write this book without which I would not have considered doing it.

His detail reviews and suggestions have helped me tremendously to finish the book until what it is today.

Secondly, DrSiraj Khan a close friend of the author, from Maslow Trainer and Management Consultantwho has allocated his precious timein givingme advice and guidance in ensuring that this book will become a fruitful effort and a reality which hopefully will serve as a guidance to up and comingHR executives and middle management staffs in carrying out their industrial relation functions effectively.

I strongly believe this book will provide a thorough insight on matters of industrial relation to all undergraduates aspiring to become successful Human Resource personnel in the future.

Yours Sincerely,

Abdul Rahman @ MaridanHjRamli.

ABOUT THE AUTHOR

Abdul Rahman @ Maridanb.HjRamli, holds a Bachelor of Science Degree (Hons) from University Malaya 1983, and MBA 2001 from University of Newport, US.

His working life span over a period of three decades whereby he served large multinational organizations such as Bando, Hitachi, TDK and Denso. He did spend about 5 years prior to that in a local based company which was MMC.

During his role as Head of Human Resource for these organizations, he frequently attendeda Globaland Regional Human Resource Conference in Thailand, Philippines and Japan. He also pioneered and lead in the execution of the PLWS in the company.

As Head of HRin the company, he was also elected to participate during the Asia Regional Climate Survey conducted atThailand in 2010.

He finally retired as a General Manager HR of Denso, and subsequently re-appointed to act as the Company HR Advisor for about a year before leaving employment to serve as a freelance HR Consultant.

During his tenure as Head of HR, he also sit as the **Panel Member of the Industrial Court of Malaysia from the year of 2001 until 2015** whereby he served some of the distinguish Chairman of the IR Court.

He believed sharing his real life experiences would benefit the young and upcoming Human Resource executives and junior Managers in this field. The objective was to give an insight in the role of managing industrial relation.

Yours sincerely and thank you

PREFACE

This book was written with the objective of sharing some of the most significance experiences that the author has underwent through in managing industrial relation.

This is not to say that those experiences were the perfect examples of what industrial relation is all about, but the author humbly hopes that it gives an insight of what to expect from the employees or union under similar kind of environments.

All the **35 case studies** were extracted from the real life experiences of the author gained during his 20 years tenure as Head of Human Resource department. The case studies were recalled, reflected and analyzed from the author's perspective, with no intention to blame any parties involved.

However, as the readers read through and understand the cases, the author hopes that it will give an insight of how each situation was resolved, or how it should have been resolved better. The decisions were made based on the essence of Industrial Relation Act which emphasize equity, good conscience and the substantial merits of the case without regards to technicality and legal form.

The author has no intention to say that, all the solutions taken were the only way to resolve the issues. Trade disputes can be resolved creatively as long as the solution is procedurally correct and legally right.

Again, I humbly apologized if the case studies written in the book offended those who were affected by it.

Sincerely,

Abdul Rahman @ MaridanHjRamli.

Chapter 1

Overall Function of Human Resource Management

As I was gazing through the window of my study room, the words of my close friend, Mr Alfred Charles keep coming back to me, "Rahman, why don't you write a book on those experiences that you have went through while managing the Human Resource function. That will be interesting." That advise is what really inspired me to write this book.

I had spent the last 20 years of my employment as Head of the Human Resource with global Multinational companies such as Bando, Hitachi, TDK, 3M and Denso. The experience and exposure to some of the world class systems and process in management was something that I could not attain in a university or college lecture room.

These experiences were priceless and I am glad to share them with the readers of this book. However, during the initial 5 years of my employment were spent in a local based company, MMC whose core business was mainly in the mining industry. This local based company had also given a wonderful and at the same time a tragic experience which I still recalled until today. That will be elaborated in the case study later.

During these three decades of employment, I underwent a lot of exciting challenges and adversity. In the process of managing the Human Resource function, it was always a challenging task to find ways to develop good HR systems and policies with the objective of creating employees who are productive, cohesive and competent with the right skills and knowledge that will help the organization to be efficient, competitive and at the same time to be an employer of choice.

Basically my role as the Head of HR function was as follows;

    i.   General administration and salary administration,

    ii.   Industrial relations,

    iii.   Union and Collective Agreement

    iv.   Employee training and development,

    v.   Compensation and benefits,

    vi.   HR Policy design, improvement and enforcement,

    vii.   Disciplinary management

    viii. Manpower planning and Recruitment,

    ix.   Leadership development and retention, and

    x.   Performance management,

The complexity of the role will depends on several factors such as the size of the workforce, nature of business, location and whether the organization is unionized or non-unionized. The larger the organization, the more complicated and complex the role of Human Resource will be. Most of the organizations that I worked for had employees of more than 1000 workers.

Apart from my focus on attaining operational excellence, the objective was to link the role towards the business point of view.

The current employment scenario is more unique as the workforce is filled up with mix a generation of baby boomers, X and Y generations. They have varied perspective and mind sets which pose a greater challenge for any HR manager to adapt in the work environment. I was consistently required to constantly evolve with the changes and adapt with the situation well.

Human resource function evolve with time

That reminded me a subject on evolution when I was studying for my basic degree in geology at the university. Accordingly, many important species extinct and disappear from the earth million years ago because of their inability to evolve with the environmental changes, whereas the crocodile were able to adapt and evolve with the continuous change of environment to survive until today.

For that reason, I have always reminded myself to be competent in adapting to the changes.

As the education level of the workforce improve, their awareness on employment rights also improve whereby a few decades ago, some organizations that practiced the unwritten policy of hire and fire may escape unscathed. Not today. Now employees are more educated and have a better awareness of their rights, and what more, the union is always there to intervene.

The workforce has understood the laws and their rights, and in this era of advance social media technology, such information is easily accessible from the internet, face book, twitter, and others.

To make it more challenging and interesting, the union is always around the corner to intervene and assist the affected workers. On the other hand, there are cases when the union presence is also necessary without which the unscrupulous companies will mistreat or exploit workers according to their whims and fancies.

Unfortunately, there were also cases when such union intervention is unnecessary and without of justification. We must bear in mind that, whether we are employer or the union, the work climate stability plays an important role in attracting FDI, or Foreign Direct Investment.

The more FDI Malaysia can attract the more employment opportunities will be created. With this in mind it is our responsibility, employer and union, to work together in creating a good working environment to promote economic growth for the betterment of the nation.

Chapter 2

Managing Industrial Relations Basic concept

In most organizations, one of the most challenging aspects of Human Resource management is managing industrial relations to create a conducive employer-employee relationship.

In a simple definition, industrial relation is a relationship between employer and employee with regards to the employment conditions of work.

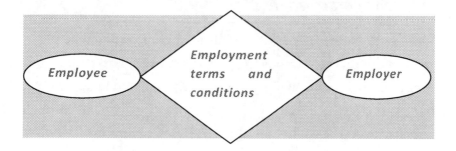

The aspect of industrial relations in any organization will pose the biggest challenge for most Human Resource department whereby the key role will be to ensure a cohesive and conducive working environment that directly supports productivity. A working environment where the employees are lacking in focus, poor morale, having lots of grievances and incompetent will hinder the efficiency of operation and the resultant productivity to the organization.

The issue of industrial relations is about a relation between an employee and employer. Issues affected can be anything from terms and conditions of employment, work related environment, safety and health, compensation and benefits and other employment related or non-employment matters.

My experiences showed that, if this industrial relationship is not managed properly, it will lead to employees' grievances and affect the function of Human Resource inevitably. It may even spill over and become a trade disputes.

Consequently this will affect the efficiency of operation which will lead to deficiency in delivery, quality, cost and productivity. This in turn affects the Profit &Loss of such organization.

Therefore, this is an important role that I had given a lot of focus and not allowed it out of my sight.

What were the tools that I had used to gauge the work climate of the organization?

During the past two decades of managing Human Resource function, here are some of the mechanisms that I had used which I would like to share with the readers. The mechanisms were mostly in placed but as we seek for continuous improvement, changes and improvement need to be made in order to stay relevance to the ever changing work environment.

Managing change is a continuous process and a journey.

Illustrated below are some of the mechanisms or tools that were used to gauge the work climate of the organization that served to reflect the health of industrial relation.

2.1 HR indicator

Some of the parameters that I had used as HR indicators are Resignation ratio, Absenteeism, Medical leave, Attendance ratio, and overtime participation percentage.

These indicators were collected on a monthly basis and such numbers would be plotted regularly and analyzed to see if the numbers show an abnormality compared to the company average or industry norms.

Experience had shown that during the periods of strain industrial relations, certain indicators will show figures above normality.

When such indication exists, I would discuss with the senior management team and watch out for any chain of reaction which may affect the organization such as loss of Productivity, Quality and Delivery or to look out for any signs of sabotage.

2.2 Direct or Formal Employees' grievances

These were grievances collected from the formal processes provided by the HR department such as Grievance form, Dialogue, Employee Care Counter and HR Care line.

Increasing numbers of such **grievances** raised by the employees is also an indication that the industrial relationship is not in a good state. It may imply that the work climate is in the negative and Human Resource department needs to analyze and understand the situation early to avoid further deterioration of the work climate.

The grievances should be analyzed and observed for any similarity or pattern that may indicate certain issues of concern which company needs to take early initiative to resolve them.

2.3 Indirect grievances

Apart from the formal grievances obtained, I had persistently advised my staffs, especially from the IR section to proactively pick up indirect grievances through management by walking around the factory.

This is a type of information obtained through informal complaints or conversation which may happen at smoking places, rest areas, during break times or any other occasions. It is therefore important that HR officer or executive to have a good relation with union and other employees in order to collect this kind of information.

Such information collected could be work related issues, safety, salary, canteen or any other matters which may cause a lot of dissatisfaction from the employees.

Small grievances if allowed to accumulate, and may lead to a big 'explosion'. This is what normally happened in many organizations which I will relate to an important case study in later chapter.

Keeping up a good Relationship with the Union

I remembered during the peak of the Collective Bargaining, one of the worksite committee told me to be aware of the picketing they would conduct the next morning. This information may not be able to stop the picketing from happening, but the good point was that, one of the members was sincere enough to warn me in advance of that incident.

The picket took place as mentioned, but management has been warned and to maintain good temperament for any provocation that might come with this incident. After all, picketing is allowed under the provision of Industrial Relations Act 1967.

2.4 Work Climate survey

This is another common tool I used to gauge the work environment of my organization.

During the several years of employment in these multinational organizations, we conducted a work climate survey during a 3-year cycle period which followed certain parameters to ensure the result reflects the actual work climate during that period of time.

Based on the data collected, the information was analyzed and countermeasures were taken to resolve problematic areas as soon as possible. Such information could be work related issues such as management, safety, victimization, salary, canteen or any other matters which may have caused a lot of dissatisfaction amongst the employees.

Identifying the Problems and Rectifying the situation.

Once the data had been gathered and problematic issues were identified, I would propose a remedy to be taken by the management in order to prevent deterioration of the working environment.

I encountered this experience in the early stages of this survey when an issue of annual increment was not remedied promptly. As a result, there was considerable abnormality on the resignation ratio of employees especially coming from junior executives who had been with company for about 2 to 3 years.

Since this was a monetary issue which the company was trying to avoid, it resulted in many resignations from this group of executives which far exceeded the industry norms. This prompted the head of departments from the key division to question the Human Resource department on the purpose of conducting the earlier survey.

They would come to me and ask blatantly,

"Rahman, what is the purpose of doing the survey if you don't proceed with improvement…you are wasting our time". Such comments came frequently and finally the top management agreed with my proposal to conduct a salary survey and propose improvements if justified to close the salary gaps.

However, it important to take notes that, not all grievances or complaints should be entertained according to employees' request, but a certain check and balance was required to ensure that the employees' welfare and benefits was reasonably looked after.

2.5 Communicating with Top Management

I would like to reflect on some of the critical incidents which took place when companies did not take seriously on proposals or recommendations made by the Human Resource department.

In reality, not all recommendations proposed by the HR head of department were easily acceptable by the top management of the Company. It took a lot of courage, patience and whatever skills that was required to convince the Managing Director to consider the proposals that was made.

In normal circumstances, for a recommendation to carry any weight and consideration, HR Head should be able to link the importance of such proposals for business priority. As for example ignoring the pleas of employees for better medical benefits and insurance package may lead to increase number of resignations.

This in turn will cause organization to lose trained and skill employees to competitors and may lose business competitiveness in the long run. To recruit and develop an employee to achieve a certain level of competence could be a long process and costly, thus it will be beneficial if such relevancy is linked to the HR initiatives for better management understanding.

I had managed to acquire such skills after many years of working in the HR field. The hard and challenging years made me wiser and matured, and that allow me to see the problems not only from the HR perspective but from business point of view.

When I was able to present the case from both perspectives, it was easier to convince the president of the company. This is an important lesson learned after many years in the job.

Looking back at those passing years, there were cases which happened as a result as an aftermath for not managing the situation accordingly. All cases mentioned below were real incidents which I had gone through during my role as Head of Human Resource.

To illustrate better, I had also included a case taken from an affiliate factory which was a subsidiary company that I was working with.

Here are some of the critical events that took place when industrial relations is not working harmoniously;

I.   Union knocking on the doors
II. High resignation rate as employees are not happy,
III. Difficulty in reaching agreement during Collective Bargaining,
IV. Lack of collaboration in company activities such as annual dinner, sports event, employees suggestion scheme and others
V.   Poor work engagement or commitment

A. Union Knocking On Company Door for Recognition

Case Study 1
Union recognition or intervention
Scenario of the Case

Many times in the past, organizations did not react positively when the employee-employer relation turn sour. Based on the experience and networks that I had with these companies, many of them panicked when the union knocks on the door seeking for recognition. The top management was aghast and hugely disappointed when the union sends a letter seeking recognition from the company.

The Managing Director of the company insisted that I arranged several meetings with the Heads of department in trying to understand the cause and finding a solution to avoid the union from coming in. To make it complicated this was also my first involvement with a national union which happened about two decades ago.

When this took place, it is almost impossible for the company to dispose the issue, unless it can be proven technically through membership verification or secret ballot –that union lacked a majority of its members who wants to join the union. This will be discussed in more detail in later chapters.

I was quite new in my involvement with the national union during the time when this issue occurred and had taken a lot of blame and accusation on the issue. There was a lot of pressure to find ways to resolve it according the expectation of the company.

How did the Company manage the situation?

Well, the company was not able to push the union away, but we managed to delay the recognition for about a year to ascertain employees who are eligible to become members of the union.

There were several visits to the Industrial Relation department office to understand the issue of union recognition and to confirm whether the request for recognition fully complied with the legal requirements.

It was finally ascertained by the Industrial relation department that the union had a majority of the employees who wanted to join the union. The company had no alternative but to accept the recognition. The whole process of recognition took almost a year to complete.

The best thing that happened to the company was, the letter of recognition was hand delivered to the General Secretary of the union. He was caught off-guard when the, company director and I, hand delivered the letter to him at his office.

Significance comments from union General Secretary

He said, "Rahman, this is the first experience for me to receive a recognition letter by hand from the company. This is nice gesture from the company, I will promise to be fair and reasonable to the company too."

His gesture and comments took us by surprise too. He kept to his promise because until today, both union and company has a reasonably good relationship.

How did the union manage to penetrate the wall of the organization?

We would never be able to go back to the time tunnel to return to where we started, but we have to proceed and live in the new chapters of living with the union. What was done cannot be undone now.

As the new chapter began, things were not the same anymore. There was a possibility of intervention from the national union if they felt their members were treated unfairly.

Of course the organization cannot always bow to all demands of employees or union, where some of its could be unreasonable at all, but by being a good listener, many issues can be resolved. One of the biggest mistakes in the past was taking things for granted.

Post-mortem analysis and management review conducted few months later revealed that when the union knocks on the door, the ground work had already existed between the interim worksite committee and the national union officials. They have worked secretly and closely behind the curtain, instigating members to join and participate in the secret ballot, and finally picked the right moment to send an official letter for recognition.

Prior to the union intervention, the union officials had been contacting the interim worksite committee, but were not able to convince the majority of the potential members. However, when a new Head of Production from the Japan Head Quarter came to take over the manufacturing Plant, scenario began to change. He had a bad temperament, managed by screaming and shouting in the meeting, and this had made many employees and even local managers to distant themselves away from him.

To worsen the scenario, the Managing director was not approachable person. As time goes by, grievances accumulated with no solution in sight. So, when the national union tried their luck again, it was a quite a smooth sailing operation.

They conducted a secret ballot meeting outside the company premises and attained the required majority. Infact the secret ballot was fully supportive of the union formation whereby 65% of the employees were in favor the union membership.

One other finding that disturbs the top management of the company was that, some local middle managers were found to support and encourage the formation of this union. However, no action was taken against them because there was no direct evidence to link them instigating the formation of the union. The situation completely changed the landscape of the work environment.

Case commentaries

As a newly promoted HR manager, I was not aware of the early symptoms simmering in the production floor, and the situation was left unattended. As a countermeasure on this issue, the management rectified all the problems identified, and created a systematic communication system for employees to voice up any of their concerns.

To collaborate and listen to the opinion or suggestion from the union, regular monthly meetings were conducted. Management began to emphasize and inculcate values of mutual respect in the organization and this helped the industrial relationship to be more stable and harmonious.

B. Sabotage on Company Operation

During the periods of severe industrial relation tensions, some of the issues that I have encountered included were;

- Increase in-house Quality defects – affecting cost of production,
- Increase external Quality defects – caused numerous customer claims, and as a result loose customers' trust,
- Regular Machines breakdown,
- Delivery failures – employees adopting work to rule, or go slow
- lack of cooperation for overtime work which resulted in man-hours and productivity lost

Case study 2
Sabotage on Product Quality
Scenario of the Case

This took place in an electronic factory that I was working in the early year of 2001. The business scenario was not encouraging but the company still managed to achieve a marginal profit.

Sometime in the middle of early January, the management team was called for an urgent meeting by the Managing Director of the company.

We were informed that several units of our products in the Customer production lines were found to be defective.

The electronic industry was very competitive and the company could not afford to have any more complaints from the major customer because any more occurrences we might lose the business

Investigation and Findings

The company reacted promptly by sending the QA team to our customer in Hong Kong to investigate the problem further. The investigation had shown that this defect was due to sabotage from the employees.

All defective products had similar characteristic that one of the copper wire was cut at the same position. Even though the quantities affected were few in numbers, but it disgraced the Company. By using a product tracking method, the company was able to narrow down the group of employees involved in made the production.

It came from the night shift, where a few of the employees who raised grievances to their supervisors about the poor salary increments they received at the beginning of the year.

Remedy or Countermeasure taken

I conducted a briefing and counseling session with this particular group of employees explaining about the defective products which happened to be produced from their group.

We made them realize on the degree of damage they had done to the company, and the possibility of company taking a severe disciplinary action against the culprits which might include dismissal.

The purpose of such briefing was to send a strong message about the impact of such sabotage and also implying that company could identify the culprits. To put the message strongly across the organization, a memorandum with regards to any form of sabotage was issued to remind employees of the severe punishment that may be inflicted for such with the misconduct which may lead ultimately to dismissal.

Commentaries

From the HR perspective, it was important to develop thrust by creating a transparent and fair appraisal system and its implementation. In this way, the employee could understand better on quantum of increment or bonus they would receive at the beginning of the year. It avoids the feeling of being exploited or victimized by the management which is fundamental to employee satisfaction.

Case study 3
Union Worksite Committee member sabotage
Training Program
Scenario of the case

As I was thinking hard to find a mechanism that could heal the relationship between HR department and the Worksite Committee, one of my staff recommended that the two teams to go for a team building training session. His idea was to use the team building session as a way to rebuild trust and understanding between the committee and management team.

I lauded the recommendation and invited the union worksite for a discussion on the idea. In the initial meeting, the idea was not easily accepted as they felt that the company had a hidden agenda behind the training program.

They were suspicious that the company may use the program to brainwash the committee members to sway to the management team during any conflicts in the future. At the same time, the union worksite committee members were also not comfortable to be seen by their members to attend such program in view of the coming Collective Agreement which was about 4 months away from the date of negotiation.

Finally the Training program was accepted

However I continued to persuade the committee members and the HQ union official about the benefits and objective of the training program. Finally, after weeks of persuasion to the parties concern, the union finally accepted to attend the training program.

The Training Section was informed about the details of the training requirement, location, and modules to be conducted during the 3 days and 2 nights program.

As we closed in towards the date, there were rumors going around the Plant that one or two worksite Committee members would not attend the program. I knew from the beginning that one or two members were making it very difficult for the program to be realized.

They were still uncertain and suspicious about the program even though it was endorsed by their own General Secretary.

The Program was sabotaged

Everything was nicely prepared; the lodgings, transportation and trainer were ready for the early morning journey to the northern state. As the management team waited for the union worksite committee members to appear, we received news from the chairman of union that they were not able to participate as 2 of their key members had decided to abandon the program.

That was really a shocking and embarrassing situation for the management team, especially HR department. We had no choice but to cancel the training program at the expense of the Company. We have paid the resort, transportation and trainers with zero return of investment.

Investigation on the Sabotage

I consulted and expressed my disappointment with the union General Secretary with regards to the last minute abandonment of training program. He was aware of it and did not endorse with that kind of behavior from his committee members. He told me to proceed with any action the company thought was reasonable.

When the investigation confirmed that the treasurer of the union committee was responsible for the fiasco, I decided to issue him a Show Cause letter for his role in instigating other committee members to abandon the training program. He admitted to the charge and apologized to the company for his behavior.

Since the misconduct was extremely serious and heard by many employees from the union group, I was in a dilemma to decide of what was the right and proper decision to make. He was actually the most vocal and influential member of the union committee, and therefore was uncertain the impact on such dismissal would bring to the process of healing the union-management relationship.

In many ways he had managed to strike worry and concern to some members of the management by being argumentative and vocal in raising many issues.

The Punishment

However, after considering all aspects of the case and the damage he had done to the training program, I proceeded to issue him with a Final Warning Letter and putting him on 6 months observation period. That decision really shocked and frightened him as he kept quiet and maintain a low profile presence over a period of 6 months. In reality I was a bit surprise by the impact of that punishment.

By the way, the punishment was lauded by the management team which they believed was correct and justified. The union treasurer who has been vocal all this while has now become quite because the warning letter had made him realized who actually his paymaster was, the company. Infact he was lucky in a way that the General Secretary had recommended me to dismiss him for his action.

Even though the company and the union General Secretary had numerous disputes on several union related matters, but I knew he was also a man with principle and integrity.

Case Commentaries

The good thing that developed from this case was; it sort of created a turning point in the union-management relationship. The union member realized that such behavior of sabotaging a company legitimate event was a bad conduct and it was not even accepted by the Union Head Quarters official. At that point of time he was left alone unprotected.

Case study 4
Refusal to Collaborate for Overtime Work
Scenario of the Case

This happened during the period of Collective Bargaining negotiation, whereby upon reaching a deadlock the union members became agitated and irritated and tried to sabotage the production target. Even though they were requested repeatedly to perform for overtime work, majority of the employees ignored the order.

The situation lasted for about a month and it affected the company and concerned the customers from the viewpoint of delivery. During this difficult period, all the executives were required to work in the production and came for the Saturday overtime work to assist in meeting customer delivery schedule.

However, when the collective bargaining was finally resolved, and production became stable; HR and head of Production retaliated by not giving overtime work to majority of the union members who boycotted the OT as a form of punishment.

Investigation and Findings

This took about 3 months and this action of denying overtime work affected the workers monetarily. Many of them came and appealed to the management to be given OT work again.

They appealed through the union worksite committee but the management stood firm until it was quite unbearable for the union committee and promised that such boycotting would not be repeated in future.

Strategic countermeasure taken by the HR department

It was a tough lesson learned by employees and the union. As for countermeasure, the company adopted a strategic recruitment plan by recruiting in more contract foreign workers who would not participate in the union activities. They enjoyed the same terms and condition as the local workers but stayed away from the union activities.

Contract foreign workers by nature of their short term employment were more focused in making as much money as possible during the short term contract of their employment in this country.

The union headquarter was not happy with the move taken by the company and raised the matter as a trade dispute which will be elaborated in later chapter.

Case study 5
Abnormal rate of resignation
Scenario of the Case

During the peak of the industrial relations distress, I have observed a high rate of resignation from the organization that I worked for, and similar trends were shown by other organizations as well.

The increase in resignation rate was not only coming from the non-executive level of employees, but also affected other levels of employees. Negative work environment can be quite infectious whereby such negative emotion can spread throughout in the whole organization.

Tense Industrial Relations Created a Negative Work Environment

I can relate an example of such a case when towards the end of collective bargaining, emotion run high amongst the union members. Both parties were taking a hard stance which stretched the collective bargaining negotiation to almost a year.

This led to several operational problems in the production floor. Some of the union members became more vocal and occasionally acted in negative manners to the superiors.

As the uneasy situation prolong, some employees felt disappointed and left the company. When more employees started to leave the company, the operation became more difficult to manage and this created a chain reaction and triggers other employees to leave as well.

C. Difficulty in Settling Collective Agreement or Disputes

During those years when industrial relations was poor, settling the Collective Agreement is always more difficult. They made it harder and made proposals which the company found difficult to agree. It can be looked as a form of retaliation in relation to the frustration they had against the company.

Case Study 6
Making THE Annual Calendar
Scenario of the Case

An example of this situation occurred while I was in the midst of preparing the Company Annual Working Calendar whereby at the same time, the Collective Bargaining dispute was referred to the Court after a long period of negotiation which ended in a deadlock.

The Company made a proposal to shift one of the public holiday to another working holiday day to improve productivity. Since the procedure of shifting the public holiday needed consent from the union worksite committee, such consent was not given by the union.

Union Disagree with Company proposal

Several discussions followed where in the last meeting the General Secretary of the union insisted the Managing Director to present himself personally in the discussion.

However, even in the presence of the Company top man, the national union still rejected the idea of the management, and consequently we were not able to shift the calendar as required. The presence of MD was just a display of union strength amongst their members.

That case reminded me and the company of how far union members could choose to be a nuisance if they wanted to.

There were also occasions in the past where the employees or the union created unnecessary issues as a form of fight back to the management to show their dissatisfaction with the management.

There were trivial issues like uniform or wearing of caps being argued by the union or their members with no concrete purpose when the real issue was their request for a higher bonus and salary increment was rejected.

This was something that HR staffs need to understand and look beyond the realm of verbal communication.

D. Lack of collaboration in company activities

I would like to relate a case whereby the union committee instigated their members not to attend the company Annual Dinner. This incident occurred due to bad blood that existed between the union and the Head of Human Resource department at that point of time.

The company and the union had a very serious friction over the Collective Agreement which ended in a deadlock, and to worsen the situation further, the Head of HR had not been an approachable person.

Refer to the case below;

Case study 7
Boycotting Company Event –Annual Family Day
Scenario of the Case

The situation took place about a few months before I joined the company. The Company had organized a grand Annual Family Day which took place at the time when the Collective Bargaining had just been declared a deadlock about a month before the event. On that fateful day, a majority of employees did not attend the event as a show of protest.

Apart from the issue of the Collective Agreement, the union was also not in good terms with the current Head of Human Resource who happened to be a very uncompromising person. Only 45% of employees attended the event which was an embarrassing situation for the management.

Investigation and Findings

A postmortem Investigation revealed that a few days before the event, there was a concerted effort by the union committee instigating the members by whispers and hand phone messages to boycott the annual event.

As the tension was still running high, the company discontinued with further investigation to avoid stretching the tension further.

Case study 8
Boycott of Company Suggestion Scheme Activity
Scenario of the Case

One of the organization that I worked for has a very strong believe in Total Quality Management system, and to support this program the company had developed an Employee Suggestion Scheme. The event had a good support and participation from employees with an average of more than 60% participation.

However, during one of the monthly Total Quality Council meeting, it was highlighted by the Secretary of the committee that there was drastic drop of monthly Suggestion scheme contribution from the employees.

Investigation and Findings

Detail analysis and discussions were carried out, and based on the findings gathered; it was discovered that there were specific reasons behind the situation. One was lack of OT due to cost down activities, while the other was a delay in concluding the Collective Agreement.

A meeting was called upon between TQM council and the union worksite committee to request for their cooperation on the Suggestion scheme contribution.

The worksite committee admitted about the issue but could not force their members to contribute as usual as this is a voluntary activity. However, they promise to appeal to their members to improve their contribution again.

The response was back to normal gradually, and the Council Committee expressed their appreciation for the cooperation given by the union committee in this matter.

2.7 How the Company could have avoid on the above cases

Knowing and Understanding the Employees' issue

The organization could have avoided the hassles of facing disputes by taking proactive action in solving employees' grievances. Human Resource department especially the IR manager should have looked into the issues and made necessary recommendations to resolve them.

Unfortunately, some HR personnel choose to ignore the situations, or were not courageous enough to report these kind of negative cases to the top management. In my years of heading the department, there are times when you need to advise or propose to the top management on doing the right things.

And to make it difficult, some senior management members were just not willing to hear this kind of issues. They are too engrossed in operational issues to extend their ears on HR matters.

Taking Prompt action to rectify problems

This is more obvious when the remedy involves monetary issues like salary or allowances. A proposal to review salary structure, annual increment, and medical benefits may not be accepted easily, or even sometimes met with negative remarks.

However, this is a continuous challenge any Head of Human Resource department need to face and convince with good facts and figures and to be supported with valid benchmarking data.

When making such recommendations, I always need to have good understanding of company business situation and priority, so that whatever is being proposed does not hurt the company financially. Understanding this principle will make HR as a true business partner of the organization.

The Challenge of Proposing for Improvement

During those years of heading the Human Resource department, I used to come across several discussions amongst other HR practitioners who voiced their frustrations of not being able to convince or failed to influence the management on recommendation made to improve the industrial relation climate of the organizations.

Many CEOs or MDs of the companies is too focused on the operation and fail to see the importance of industrial harmony. Some recommendations proposed by the HR department were ignored or there is difficulty in getting the acceptance from the top management.

There were even cases where the Head of HR were not courageous enough to proceed with their recommendations. Recommendation for improvement is important to bring change and transform the organization to become a better work place not only for the workers but the whole organization.

The Importance of Cooperation and Understanding from the Top Management

A harmonious work environment creates a happy and healthy workforce, which will improve the followings;

- Collaboration and teamwork,
- Engagement or focus
- Better employee retention, and
- Productivity and quality output

During one of the board meeting with all directors I had a few years ago, I was asked the question of, "Rahman, what did you learn during the last CA negotiation..." and my reply was, "it was quite unfortunate that I was not able to influence the top management on certain decisions during the Collective bargaining".

There were moments of silence after I answered that question, probably they were not expecting that kind of answer from me.

Actually what happen during that time was, there were certain issues that could have wrapped up the Collective Bargaining. However, the inability of the top management to agree on matters of common sense resulted in the Collective Agreement being referred to the Industrial Court. That was quite unfortunate.

Lesson Learned

However that was a bitter lesson learned by the company. For subsequent Collective Bargaining negotiation recommendation from HR department were accepted with relative ease

In order to ensure whatever recommendations made are justifiable and fair, Human Resource department should be cautious on the monetary impact to the organization.

As a business partner to the organization, HR personnel should always link the proposal to the impact it will have on the operation o the company.

Chapter 3

Integrity and Fairness: Impact on Industrial Relation

As the organization moves forward to achieve business expansion and to stay competitive, the elements of employee of satisfaction and productivity become a crucial success factor to the organization. The organization needs to create the right working environment that enhances employee morale and productivity.

Therefore it is the role of HR to find or develop a conducive working environment that raises satisfaction, morale and motivation which in turn improve productivity.

The challenge of creating a conducive working environment relates to many aspects of human resource management which can be summarized as follows;

- Terms and conditions of employment,
- Values and culture of the organization,
- Union management and industrial relationship,
- Team spirit,
- Training and development, and
- Rewards system

In a unionized organizations, the aspect of building good relations with the union becomes an important factor that employer need to focus. Failure in doing this will attract unnecessary problems to the organization.

Some organizations thought that paying a good monetary package to the employees was good enough to attain employee satisfaction, but in actuality there are other elements that can also affect the work environment. There are also other reasons to this, and probably this could be due to lack of team spirit or negative work cultures, or even poor leadership that drives the employees away.

However, my case study in this chapter will try to focus and reflect on the importance of building good industrial relations in the organization, with a special focus on union management relationship. In the process of creating the right working environment, I would emphasize on the following matters;

a) Prevention of Conflicts, and

b) Rectification or Countermeasures

3(A) Prevention of Conflicts

Allowing dissatisfaction and complaints to simmer within the production floor and getting hotter by the day is a dangerous act. The Human Resource department should have picked up the grievances through the indicators designed and find a solution, and communicate to the senior management of the Company.

The top management of the company should have been informed on the status of the company industrial relation climate on a regular basis. Any negative situation may affect the business of the company, and finally the bottom line of the organization will be affected.

Here are some of the recommendations proposed, but these are by no means exhaustive;

i. Regular Health Check on the Work Climate

This will give the overall picture of employees' satisfaction towards the management and HR department. Some organizations employ an external consultant to conduct the Work Climate Survey, whilst others conduct it internally. Conducting through an external party is a better option because the survey will avoid impartiality and allow better judgment to be made.

Communicating the Activity

Prior to conducting such work climate survey, the union officials should be informed on the objective and selection method to be used. This is to show management transparency and ensure that the union members support the initiative taken by the company.

The result of the climate survey shall serve as a Work Climate indicator in the organization. Issues that are weak need to be improved immediately because unhappy work environment could jeopardize company operation and productivity in the long run.

Some of these matters could arise from canteen management, company transport, uniforms, and harassment by superiors, monetary issues, attitude of management, favoritism and others.

ii. Regular Communication

This will allow the employees to raise any of their concerns, opinions, or on matters that relates to their working environment. Regular communication can be done through;

a) **Monthly Employee dialogue** between management and selected employees,

b) **Union management dialogue** on monthly basis,

c) Setting up a regular **HR counter** to hear any grievances, enquiry or any issues from employee and on a one to one basis,

d) **Communication Box** which will serve to hear employees complaints in a confidential manner,

e) **Departmental dialogue**

For a unionized organization it is advisable that the union committee members be required to participate in all the committees that was set up by the company. As for example, I had to ensure that at least one of the union worksite committee members to sit in most of the committee set up by company such as Cafeteria committee, Safety and Health Committee, TQM council committee, Annual Dinner and others.

In this way, the union will be updated on the information and counter measures taken by the company. And this should make them answerable to their members for any new development in the organization.

Identifying Priority issues

Some issues that repeat in the process of communication indicate genuine issues that need to be resolved speedily. As for example, when the issue of cafeteria is being raised at all or most dialogue sessions, it shows that this issue is genuine and requires prompt solution from the Company.

The importance of allowing the employees to speak up and be heard is very important in any organization. When such avenue is rare and difficult to find, employees will express such frustration on the wall of toilets, sabotage product quality, angers flare up, low attendance and etcetera.

Case study 9
Picketing and Illegal Strike
Scenario of the Case

This happen to large Electronic Multi-National Company which was affiliated to the organization that I worked for. The HR manager is close friend of mine. During the mid-90s, when electronic companies were allowed to form an in-house union, this company did not have this type of union yet. The company was doing well, producing good quality products and with very few issues of customer complaints.

The employees knew the situation as it was the practice of this company to present the annual business performance which included profit and loss. However, many of the employees were not happy with the basic terms and conditions provided, and the most glaring one was the annual increment.

Grievances Taken for Granted by the Management

The annual increment was indeed far below the average increment within that industrial area. The issues were raised on many occasions available to the employees, but were ignored or taken for granted by the top management in the hope that such grievances were short lived. Experience in the past has shown that assumptions are a risky option to choose.

Slowly the operation began to deteriorate and began to experience poor quality, bad delivery, poor productivity and mysterious machines breakdown during the night shifts. Investigation conducted revealed that this was mainly due to employees' dissatisfaction with the company and this was a show of disappointment to the company. It was too late when the final blow came.

Employees went on Illegal strikes!

It was early morning, in the year 1989 when the company was shocked by a major illegal strike outside the company premises.

Urgent meetings and appeals made by the management team asking the employees to come back to work failed. It was a catastrophe which lasted for a about two weeks and needed external intervention from relevant officials from Ministry of Human Resource to resolve the trade dispute.

Urgent investigation was conducted to understand the reasons behind the huge show of dissatisfaction, and it was discovered that the final explosive display of behavior was contributed by accumulation of dissatisfactions raised many times earlier which were not taken seriously by the HR department.

Issues such as food provided at the canteen, transportation, allowances, salary increments and frequent harassment by superiors were not being resolved and taken seriously by HR department. As a result these frustrations simmered underground like lava waiting to burst into a huge explosion.

This negative event has a huge impact to the overall working environment and it took a long time to reconcile the strained relationship and trust lost. It also led to the formation of an in-house union in the company.

Findings

The findings revealed that, apart from the issues mentioned above, it also pointed out that HR department was not sensitive and caring enough towards the problems of the employees.

This is an area where every IR manager should pay attention and take proactive countermeasures to avoid such grievances from reaching an unbearable level in the organization.

It was a bitter lesson learned by the company and became a landmark case to be remembered and referral for future improvement. It was sad that many of the ring leaders who lead the illegal gathering and picketing were dismissed from the company. Probably it was a necessary decision during the crisis.

Remedy

Finally an in-house union was set-up and a regular meeting was conducted to allow better communication between the employee and the employer.

I just happened to come across with one of the leaders many years later who was already working as an assistant manager of production in one of the manufacturing company in the nearby area. He seemed to be polite and much focused on his job, implying that, he could have done quite well in the previous company if the working condition was right.

What the Company could have done to avoid this situation?

Employees are important assets to any organization. However in the era of cost cutting measures, many organizations ignored the pleas of employees for better living conditions and as a result, sour the industrial relations between the two parties.

The situation could have been worse if an external union was to be set-up in the organization. Instead of managing the situation internally, the issues would be dragged to become a trade dispute. This could go on to the industrial court which would cost money and time to the organization. In the process it sours the industrial relations climate between the management and union.

This will affect employee focus and commitment in the job which have an impact on overall productivity and efficiency of the company.

The Head of Human Resource department could have saved the situation by monitoring work climate and checked the depth of employee of dissatisfaction. What were the priority issues, and find ways to resolve them speedily and conduct annual salary and benefits benchmarking, and try to close the gaps when the situation is too far from the industry standard or norms.

iii. Integrity and Fairness in making decision

In any organization the issues of integrity and fairness cannot be taken lightly. Many times in the past, organizations fail to earn employees' respect and trust because many of the decisions they made fail to show fairness and is tainted by malicious intentions.

Such decisions are very sensitive, as for example, in evaluating employees' performance or inflicting disciplinary punishment which lacks reasonableness or is disproportionate from viewpoint of the employees. All these action will be viewed with suspicion by employees.

In a more serious situation, making decision which affects employees' livelihood such as downgrading, demotion or dismissal will be more crucial for the company to decide fairly and correctly.

Organization should be more cautious and ensure the process is done in a transparent manner and procedurally compliant.

In a unionized environment, such decisions will be scrutinized by the union officials and if they felt such decision is unfair to their members, a grievance complaint will be filed to the company. This lack of credibility and ethics by the management team, will damage the union-employer relationship.

Case study 10
Abuse of Authority by Chairman of the Canteen Committee
Scenario of the case

This was the case about the Chairman of Company Cafeteria committee who abused his authority by asking or forcing the cafeteria owner to give him money on a regular basis.

In doing so, he closed his eyes on the poor management of the cafeteria owner which resulted in the deterioration of quality of service and foods to an unbearable level for the employees. He continuously overlooked and ignored the opinion and complaints from the committee members and employees.

In the process there were frequent heated arguments between the union committee, cafeteria committee and the Chairman which caused some committee members to resign their position.

He just vetoed whatever decisions made by the committee. The union even threatened to picket or raise the issue as a trade dispute but I insisted on a time frame to resolve the problem.

Investigation and Findings

To avoid further escalation of the issue, I initiated an investigation on the case by taking statements from various persons in the company. The thorough investigation had confirmed the previous suspicion that he was taking monies from the caterer as well from the company vendors. They had to give him the money as failure to do so; chairman of the committee threatened to terminate his catering contract.

However, before any disciplinary action could be taken against him, I called for an inquiry in order to ensure justice and legal compliance is accorded to the accused. This is holding to the principle of natural justice

"No man shall be condemned unheard, until he is proven guilty as charged".

Admission of Guilty to the Allegations

I was quite shocked that during the inquiry he admitted to all the charges, and ultimately found him guilty. Based on my discussion with the managing director, we decided to dismiss him without notice.

On the day of sending the dismissal letter to him, I went to his house with one of my executive, and was saddened to see his sons running in the rain not knowing that his father was just about to be fired from his job. The Cafeteria committee Chairman was also the Assistant QA manager of the company.

After that episode, the Cafeteria committee went through a restructuring process and a proper written policy and guidelines was put in place to ensure that it would safeguard the committee from any similar incident in the near future.

Commentaries and Reflection of the Case

The case had no complexity from the view of law and process. The positive impact from that dismissal was, it displayed the management fairness and integrity in dealing with the issue of abusing one's authority.

Actually prior to my employment in the company, the chairman of the cafeteria committee was a very close friend of my predecessor at that point of time. This was where the problem started. The situation had made him 'untouchable' in the eyes of other employees.

When he was finally dismissed, it opened the eyes of the employees and union that, as the new Head of HR department, I would not tolerate this kind of character, be it coming from a senior staff of the management or member of the union.

The case had improved the image of HR department and enhanced its integrity and credibility in the eyes of the employees.

Case study 11
Harassment of subordinates by a superior
Scenario OF THE case

In this case, an assistant manager was reported to have harassed his subordinates repeatedly by using a vulgar words and harsh instructions. Employees who questioned his instruction were threatened or given bad evaluation at the end of the year.

Few grievance forms were issued but were not forwarded to the respective department Head and consequently came to the point whereby the national union intervened and expressed their disappointments towards the company, especially the HR department.

Investigation and Findings

The truth was that, this situation had never reached the HR department. It was kept under the carpet by the section Head in the hope that it would fade away with time. That was the initial thinking of that particular superior and section Head. He was too egoistic and adamant, thus refused to bow down by any pressure imposed upon him by his own section Head or his workers.

The working environment in the section was severely jeopardized whereby as a consequence there were lots of quality rejects, late delivery and poor cooperation on OT work.

During this period, there was tension in the work environment, and when the union worksite committee intervened, the situation had spiraled out of control.

Remedy

As the Head of HR department, I was not aware until that point of time and was definitely embarrassed and irritated. During the meeting with the union committee, they expressed their disappointment with the attitude of the department Head who they believed collaborated in keeping the employee's grievances under the carpet.

The vice-chairman of the committee raised his voice in the meeting and said, "En Rahman what was HR doing, and how can we protect our members from the attitude of this type of superior, we are really disgusted." The heated arguments occurred in the presence of the affected workers and superior, plant director, and HR personnel.

It took several meetings later to close the case, where the superior concern agreed to apologize and promise not to repeat similar behavior in the future. To ensure such behavior was not repeated, this particular superior was put under close observation by the Human Resource department.

In order to improve and maintain the new environment, the situation was monitored by his section Head and HR personnel closely. I visited the worksite occasionally and had an informal talk with the employees and the superior.

Case commentary

Subordinates harassment occur in all sorts of working environment. This type of behavior cannot be allowed or tolerated in any organization because it jeopardizes the working environment and which in turn affects efficiency and productivity. When such incident happened, it shaken the trust the employees had towards their superior.

Trust and amicable relationship grew with time, and even though bad blood will heal with time and effort, the scars will always be there and there is always a possibility for friction to appear if either party is not careful.

Fairness and Integrity

Appraisal Evaluation—unfair employee appraisals

One of the key HR processes which will drive any organization will be the Performance Management System or PMS in short. This process is crucial in nurturing and retaining good performing employees in the organization which in turn help the company to maintain competitiveness in the global market.

It was a fate or destiny that on many occasions, the early stage of my entry into most companies would be to faced challenges that need to be resolved fast. One of these was an issue of strong biasness or favoritism in the implementation of PMS.

There were numerous complaints about biased or unfair performance evaluation practiced by superiors. In fact this issue had surfaced during the Work climate survey that was conducted prior to my employment here.

I was entrusted and challenge by the management to bring back confidence, transparency and integrity in this importance human resource system. When the system is properly managed it can drive the organization to become more productive and efficient which is crucial to develop a high performing organization.

The Scenario of the Situation

Many employees expressed their disappointment with what they believed as an unfair evaluation process conducted by their superiors. They had seen cases of low performance or problematic employees being given a better evaluation which was reflected through better annual increment or bonus.

As a result, at many meetings and dialogue sessions conducted, the issue of unfair or bias evaluation was repeatedly highlighted by the employees.

Some of the similar questions rose;

"En Rahman, I don't think the company need to implement the appraisal system anymore because at the end of the year, it is the same guy who got the good bonus and increment." or "En Rahman, how come my annual bonus is so poor when the other guys with disciplinary problems achieved better than me".

Such grievances on the appraisal system had develop a sense of mistrust towards the management, and it took huge effort and time to reconcile the situation.

Case study 12
Unfair Appraisal Evaluation
Scenario of the Case

At the end of each appraisal period around middle of December of each year, I would gather and summarize the findings of each division appraisal ratings and analyzed the data closely. One of my duties would be to scrutinize and validate the evaluation by respective department heads before bringing it to the board of Directors meeting for the final approval.

Investigation and Findings

As I went through the full appraisals received from all departments, I began to see the truth of unfair Appraisal Evaluation. There were employees with poor disciplinary records or attendance that were astonishingly given a "Good" rating.

The policy was clear on the disciplinary issue, whereby employees who fell short within a certain disciplinary level would automatically be rated as "Poor". All department Heads had been reminded of this policy prior to the start of the period which was part of my strategy to eradicate the problem of unfair evaluation.

Some employees who receive lower marks were given a higher rating, whilst a few of those with high marks were given lower ratings. This was a very obvious unfair treatment on performance appraisal done by some superiors. The yearend rating is a very important Human Resource process because it has a direct impact on employees' annual increment, bonus and promotion.

Remedy or Action Taken to Resolve the Issue

In order to rectify the issue, I raised a strong objection and returned back the affected files to the respective department Heads for correction. The stern request was commended positively by the Managing Director.

A follow up memorandum to all department Heads was issued to remind them about this unethical evaluation and advised for the necessary rectification. In the process some department Heads or Directors adamantly tried to justify the evaluation of their subordinates, but HR stood firm based on the policy of the company.

The firm stance taken by HR caused few red faces in the process. They were not used to be challenged or resisted before and whatever was done, normally passed through without any hassle about it.

Based on the feedbacks from the long service HR staffs such behavior had been going on for quite sometimes, and no serious effort or countermeasures was taken to correct the problem. Some superiors abused their authority and damage the trust of employees on the system.

Winds of Change

I had to intervene on this negative culture as it jeopardized the work environment and weaken the trust of employees towards the management. Therefore, to continue with the winds of change, continuous reminders through meetings and dialogues were conducted to emphasize on the importance of fair evaluation. Section heads were given refresher training on the system.

This effort brought gradual improvements, and slowly the grievances on unfair performance appraisal diminished after about two years. My effort was also commended by the union members as they could see the winds of change from the results of such appraisals.

The union became more supportive of the appraisal system as they believe the issue of favoritism can finally be erased from the process of implementation. This in fact had raised the image of the Human Resource department in the eyes of the union.

Lesson Learned

During the period prior towards embarking on the counter measures, many employees actually had lost trust on the PMS and consider it as a mockery of the system. As process owner of the reward system, I had to remedy and revamp the implementation to ensure there would be no injustice done in evaluating employees' work performance.

This is management of change and I had to design a strategy to ensure a proper adoption of the PMS finally takes place. The importance of fairness and integrity is crucial to create trust and good collaboration from the employees. Once the change had been triggered, the next step will be to keep the momentum striving for consistency and fair play.

Let's see a guiding quote on the importance of fairness and integrity from one of great leader, Dwight D.Eisenhoweron who said;

"Though force can protect in emergency, only justice, fairness, consideration and cooperation can finally lead men to the dawn of eternal peace."

Case study 13
Overtime Payment not fulfilled
Scenario of the case

In this case a group of employees were required to attend a Safety training session during one of the Saturday which was supposed to be a non-working day for the employees. The employees had refused to attend unless they were paid an overtime for the full one day session.

Since the training session was one of the requirement in the Safety and Health policy, the employees were required to attend with a promise by the section superior that, instead of paying them an allowance, they would be paid OT.

The Superior was not aware that, the Training department would only pay such training attendance based on Allowance as stipulated in the policy.

The change in the payment from Allowance to OT rate was not communicated to the Training department and as a result was rejected when the claim was made a week after the training session was completed. This was in accordance to the Training policy of the company.

When the news of OT rejection came to the notice of the affected employees, there was a huge uproar and disappointment accusing the company of not honoring the promised made earlier.

The union demanded explanation from their superior as to why the promise made earlier was not kept by the section. They were adamant that their members to be paid an OT rate as promised but such demand was firmly rejected by the Training section Head.

Tensions Running High in the Company

The union worksite committee requested my intervention in this issue and to resolve it according to what was promised earlier. I conducted several meetings with the related section and union worksite committee to understand the situation and find a fair solution to resolve the issue amicably.

This was quite a difficult situation for either side as it was a conflict between principle and company policy. The Training department was not willing to accept the OT claim and adamantly wanted to stick strictly to the policy of the company which was correct.

The union on the other hand argued that their members would not have attended the training but did on the promise of OT payment. They even provided several witnesses who attended the meeting where such was promises were made earlier.

Intervention of Union Head Quarter

The union General Secretary intervened by writing a nasty and negative letter to the Managing Director and me accusing the company of being unethical in its conduct of treating their members.

During this period of negotiation, tension was running high and so were operational issues. It had became a company problem as the national union demanded the issue to be settled in their favor or raise the issue as a trade dispute to the Industrial Relation Department.

Remedy

I organized a few meeting sessions with the Head of Training department, Corporate Director and MD of the company to find a reasonable solution to this conflict. Finally, the management agreed to comply with the promise made by the superior and paid the employees based on overtime rate.

To protect the policy in future, a memorandum with regards to the special acceptance was issued to all employees and department Heads. A copy was sent to the union Head Quarters for their acknowledgment.

The company felt that by putting a strong and clear stance about the decision will not let the employees to feel that the balance of power is shifting to the union. A decision on the operational issues was still a company prerogative.

Case commentaries

It opened the eyes of everyone in the company that the management should not take promises for granted, especially when it was made towards the union members.

It is not to accuse that the union members are unreasonable, but they come to work and earn a living and will do their best to bring home every dollar earned from the hard work they put in.

In a working environment, promises made are often seen as **a verbal contract** especially when it is conveyed to the subordinates. Therefore it is especially important for superiors and management not to make promise unless you are definitely sure it can be done.

Lesson Learned

There were cases in the organization where superiors made a promise to promote an employee, but when the time comes for the promotion, this particular employee was left in the cold. What happen next? The employee resigned or if he stays on, he will spread unfavorable remarks about his superior.

Promises made must, as a matter of principle be kept by the Company.

Chapter 4

Trust is the essence of Industrial Relation

During the three decades of my employment, I was fortunate to have the opportunity to work in a various working environments. The most exciting and challenging roles came during my tenure as the Head of Human Resource in one of the largest automotive manufacturer in the world.

It was during this time that I had endured fascinating and at the same time turbulent years in the role that tested my ability to the limit, not only as HR personnel but also as a person.

I believe sharing this experience was very important as it will provide an insight to readers and probably use them as guidance in your role as HR practitioner.

4.1 Managing a Unionized Company.

When I came to the company, I was uncertain about the kind of environment that I was going into. I joined the company through a headhunting agency which briefed me about this huge and wonderful organization. I was told by the headhunter that the company has a national union and was looking for someone who has the ability and experience to manage it. At that point of time I am not too sure whether I had the right competencies for the job. The rest is history.

I knew later that a few of my predecessors come and left the company after a short stint in the job. Why they left is something that I would not want to elaborate here. This company had a national union which was formed about 25 years ago and the 6th Collective Agreement was almost expiring.

As I discovered later, the company had just gone through a bitter relationship with the union and the working climate was far from harmonious. In order to understand better, I would share this experience based on the sub-topics below;

a.   Understanding the current challenges and culture
b.   Building trust and relationship

4. 1.1: Understanding the Current Challenges and Work Culture

During the early days in my job, the industrial relationship was far from harmonious due to the bitter relationship the union had with the previous Head of HR department. I would not put the entire blame on my predecessor as I was told, she did not have the working experience in a manufacturing environment prior to joining this organization.

There was a lot of hatred and distrust from the employees towards the management, especially with the HR department. So when I came in, there was a lot of question marks from the staffs, as well as expectations from the management and whether I am the right person to resolve the existing negative relationship.

As I went through the past one year history, some of the negative issues that I would like to share are as follows;

I.   Some union members were boycotting company events such as Annual Dinner and Sports Activities,

II.   Sabotage of operation through quality problems, refusal to do OT during busy periods,

III. Poor cooperation as for example on the Improve Suggestion scheme – a drastic drop of employees participation,

IV.   Behaving negatively and displayed elements of aggression during official meetings, and

V.   Filing grievance forms at the slightest issue

The working atmosphere was still negative and even though the communication channels were properly in place, it could not rectify the situation.

As I went through the early periods of adjustment, there were several issues or complaints brought up by the employees, and some of these were favoritism in the Year-End appraisal such as incentive, promotion, bonus, and unfair treatment for disciplinary punishment, OT allocation, work safety, uniforms and some others.

Understanding the Work Environment in Detail

In order to understand the gist of the problems, I developed a close relationship with the union worksite committee members and kept a regular communication with them. To understand better, numerous discussions and meetings were conducted with section and department heads to understand from the two sides of a coin.

This information gave me a good understanding on the root cause of the problem. I was fortunate that the Company had conducted a Work Climate survey 2 years earlier, thus it was a great help for me to understand the weak points of the organization.

From the analysis made and information gathered, it was quite obvious that Human Resource department was the weakest point that contributed to the problems of this relationship.

Findings

It took me by surprise with these findings and began to ponder if I could gather enough strength and energy to bring changes to this negative perspective and work environment which had embedded in the minds of employees. This requires a mindsets reversal as well as paradigm shift.

Well, as I got closer to the key issues of employees dissatisfaction, I made a strong intent to improve trust on HR department. Urgent employees issues where possible were resolved as speedily as possible. This was important to create a competent and dependable image of the department.

However, adhoc conflicts with the union were unavoidable during the period as they always had intention to put the new Head of HR to the challenge. This was something that I had to be prepared.

Issues of Conflicts

The union would show a lot of resistance or disputes on many issues such as uniform distribution, cafeteria, changing working shifts, OT allocation and etcetera. It was a show of union power to the company and especially towards me as the new HR head coming into the organization.

As I displayed consistency, fairness and ethics in making decisions, the sense of trust began to grow which augurs well for relationship building. There were cases, when HR needed to agree with the union, as for example in complying with the right process of Performance Linked Wages system.

Some supervisors were still found to exercise favoritism and not complying to the procedure as required. This has created much disappointment amongst the employees. I took a serious note on this complaint and called meetings with the related department heads to voice this issue.

Managing Conflicts

However, similarly I showed disagreement with the union members for not cooperating for OT requirements during the peak season which affected delivery to major customers. On both types of meetings, the employees were told to understand that, business and operational decision will remain a company prerogative.

That was one of the difficult parts to make the union worksite committee understand the limitation of the union scope and responsibility. They were confused on the interpretation of the word 'consultation' and 'getting consent'. They believed that those words were the same, and this was the challenge that I had to overcome, and consequently led some conflicts in the initial stage.

Understanding on Management Prerogative

Putting back the right understanding of company prerogative and interpreting correctly on the rights of employees based on the Collective Agreement were done slowly but continuously. At the initial stage it was painful as the union took every opportunity to argue consistently with the management.

I took great pains to control the meetings or adhoc discussions with the objective to avoid an outburst into aggressive arguments.

Slowly but surely, as the time went by, with persistence and continuous trust building, the relationship began to improve. Meetings became more relaxed and much laughter could be seen, and the union began to listen more during the meetings.

After more than 3 years down the road, the relationship became too close that the worksite committee decided to leave the national union and form an in-house union.

However this intention was not fully accepted by some of the members and their intention was leaked to the General Secretary of the union who made a drastic effort to prevent this from happening. I was neutral on their intent to form an in-house union.

4. 1.b Building Trust and Relationship

The importance of Maintaining Good communication

Communication

Once the organization had attained a stable and conducive work environment, the next challenge is to sustain it and move on to the next level for better work commitment, engagement, loyalty and good overall discipline.

In order to sustain or improve on the relationship, I had put in a lot of effort into improving communication to ensure employees were informed on matters of the company or any changes that will affect the terms and conditions of their employment.

This could be matters on safety issue, products changes, production layout, business performance and direction, new HR system and process and other similar things of their concern.

Communicating effectively

Effective communication is the process of accurately forming a message, sending it and it being completely understood by the recipients. Effective communication requires the synergy between verbal and nonverbal that is, body language, gestures and actions that agree with one another.

It will not do any good if a manager verbally says he is interested in the employees' suggestions but never creates a way or opportunity for employees to express their thoughts. The messages will contradict each other. This leads to confusion and frustration.

During the early stage of Performance Linked Wages System introduction, there was a lot of misunderstanding especially during it's implementation, and as a result there were several complaints made against the superiors accusing them of being unfair.

To resolve and cushion the impact of the change and prevent the confusion, I conducted several training sessions for the management, union worksite committee and direct employees.

On another occasion, there were a lot of grumbling in the production floor whereby many supervisors were not happy with their existing terms and conditions especially on matters like annual salary increment.

In such a situation, it was pertinent that Human Resource department called for a meeting with affected employees to understand their points of concerns and giving opportunity for them to talk directly to Head of HR department.

The method on how the companies will rectify the problem is not too critical, but it is imperative that the employees are given an early opportunity to speak up and be heard.

During the earlier years of my stint as Head of HR department, I was a bit naïve for not being able to see the significance of communication. As a result it triggered the set-up of a national union.

It is not to say that the formation of union is a hugely sinful matter from the management perspective, but many companies would try their best to stay away from it. There were cases, when the existence of union helped to bring equilibrium to the working climate in some organizations.

The Importance of Communicating Changes to Employees

In order to keep with the continuous improvement and enhance organizational effectiveness, I would conduct changes in the Human Resource systems, policy or process. Communicating for change is not an easy thing to do, especially when the employees are affected.

I would like to share a few case studies examples where communicating the issue can be quite difficult;;

a)   Revising and changing of Recruitment policy,
b)   Implementing the PLWS system,
c)   Punctuality,

Case study 14
Changing the Recruitment Policy
Scenario of the Case

The issue of revising the policy was triggered during the process of year-end performance evaluation during the year. It was always during this time that the issue of favoritism came to light when close relatives were also the superiors conducting the evaluation. The result of the year end evaluation became the focal point as it would affect increment, bonus and promotion.

Reasons for Change

To prevent the possibility of conflict of interest during evaluation in future, I reviewed and revised the policy accordingly. This would prohibit any employment of close relatives within the same division or department, and those relatives who were already in the same department will be issued a letter of transfer to another department. The policy created a huge uproar and dislike from all categories of employees who were affected.

Since this policy is important in establishing integrity and fairness, I moved forward with its implementation. I had to bear the grumbles and dissatisfaction of employees either from the union or non-union.

A few relatives who tried to find jobs within the same department or division in the company were rejected and certain employees were transferred out from existing department to another because he or she had a close relative to the department or division head.

Resistance to Change

The union raised their dissatisfaction with the policy, and questioned the necessity of doing the change, to which I had explained several times before. It was during one of the meeting that I reminded the union on the rights of the organization to operate and manage its business operation in all aspects as clearly mentioned the **Collective Agreement** which is stated as follow;

"Article 5: The union recognizes the rights of the Company to operate and manage its business in all aspects."

The change also raised eyebrows with some managers as they were not comfortable with it. Some of the managers lose their reliable staffs to other departments as a consequence of the new policy.

Remedy and Action Taken

During the period of transformation, several meetings were conducted to explain on the justification of the policy. There were always arguments questioning the justification for HR to conduct the change. It was a stressful period for me and HR department to stand firm on the principle that you believe is correct.

The communication process was always difficult as the employees would put a strong resistance but this is where I need to show persistent in delivering the right message.

> Case study 15
> Implementing a performance linked waged system
> Scenario of the case

During settlement the of 6th Collective Agreement, one of key decision of the Court Award was the introduction of Performance Linked Wages System, or PLWS. It was in the early part of 2006 where such system was still quite new in the industry.

It has been 2 years of struggle when the proposal was finally approved and came to realization through a Court award.

During early days when it was introduced and proposed, the system of PLWS was initially rejected by the union as they did not want a system that can push their members to achieve higher productivity.

In the earlier format, increment and bonus were equal for all direct employees, and it did not differentiate or motivate employees towards higher productivity. So by putting this system in place, it created a competitive environment in the workplace.

Showing Resistance to Change

As expected, during the initial stage of implementation, the employees showed strong resistance and tried to find weaknesses of the PLWS system. Several complaints of a trivial nature were unnecessarily highlighted to the HR department.

It took several meetings, presentations and trainings to communicate about the benefits of the PLWS system. There were times when I was challenged by both sides of the camp on the PLWS issue, the union and management.

The worksite committee consistently highlights the problems created by the PLWS. Some of these problems were;

- Some Superiors give their own rating without conducting the necessary face to face interview with subordinates,
- Rating given were dubious with no proper justification,
- Rating was changed for the worse behind the back of employees,
- In many cases appraisal interviews were not conducted

As the transformation was necessary, I have to be persistent and patient in listening to the continuous protest or complaints given by the union. Unfortunately as I looked and studied the issue, some of the complaints highlighted were found to be true.

Remedy Taken

In order to proceed effectively, and move forward with the implementation of the new PLWS system, the mistakes or weaknesses were corrected. They were reminded that not complying with the PLWS would be treated as non-compliance of the Court award.

The union finally realized that, the Human Resource department was fair with both level of employees and began to show trust in the new system.

It was a continuous struggle all the way but persistence, sincerity and trust finally won the day for me in the process of implementation.

Case study 16
Raising the Bar on Punctuality
Scenario of the Case

One day as I sat in the management meeting with the Board of Directors, suddenly one of the Directors voiced his concerns that the some executives were not punctual on their return to the work place after each break time.

He opined that this behavior needed to be stopped and punctuality needed to be maintained for better discipline and productivity.

Background of the case

This was indeed true. Consequently, I was asked by the Board of Directors to take a lead on this subject and find ways to improve the situation quickly. In actuality, the executives of the company have been taking extra break of 5 to 10 minutes after each break time either to smoke or take another cup of coffee at the vending machines.

This has been going on for quite a while with the understanding that the executive's work time should be a bit flexible to suit their working requirement.

There were many instances that meetings had to cross the break time due to urgency in making decisions or they worked extra hours after 5.00 pm to meet customer's delivery needs.

Of course when the news came to the executives, many were disgusted with the lack of top management understanding in this matter. I had meetings with them to explain the rationale and justification of timekeeping after every break time.

Points of Concern

This is the period where HR department need to strike a good balance of listening to employees' grievances but at the same time to stay firm on the issue of punctuality.

The essence of communication should contain sincerity of the issue and the reasons of raising the bar.

Again to make the change, a grace period was given to cool down the heat of disagreement and giving the employees' time for the paradigm shift to take effect positively.

However something happened in the process.

As I reminded the top management such changes would take time, it was unfortunate that one of the Directors was not patient enough to wait for the improvement.

As it happened, this particular Plant Director went to the cafeteria during the afternoon break and stood watching at the employees who were still rushing to finish their hot cup of tea or soup. Not finished with his antics; he went further by showing his watch to the nearest employees who happened to be the Chairman of the union worksite committee and with few other employees.

Employees and union Reaction

This caused the employees concerned to be so embarrassed by the incidents and came to see me the next day.

They told me firmly, "En Rahman, we know about the punctuality issue, but do you think Mr. Abc showing his watch to us while we were drinking coffee was right? And do you think that 10 minutes break time is really enough when queuing to get the coffee alone took us about 5 minutes."

I told him to be patient and will look into this matter seriously. I had a meeting with the Director concern and advise him not to do it again; otherwise some employees might react negatively. I had also advised the union to stay away from doing anything foolish to avoid any unwanted incidents which they might regret later.

Remedy Taken

After a series of meetings with the union and executive members of the Company, the top management accepted my advice that the improvement required the company to look at other aspects as well, and hopefully raising the bar on punctuality would come slowly but surely.

When the chaotic situation finally settled down, the campaign began to take off effectively. There were elements of respect and trust which made it easier for everyone to collaborate.

Lesson Learned

Many organizations looked at communication just as another basic requirement without really putting in much effort to ensure the essence and process of communication become effective. Failure to deliver the right message leads to misunderstandings which further escalate employees' grievances or dissatisfaction to a new level.

Communication styles or techniques depend on its purpose. During my tenure as Head of Human Resource we developed communication channels for the employees to voice up their concerns and opinions to improve understanding and work collaboration. Some of the examples which were mentioned earlier are as follows;

- Employee dialogue session,
- Improvement suggestion scheme,
- Monthly union management meeting,
- Monthly industrial relations care counter, and
- Employee suggestion box

These are some of the formal communication channels given to employees to speak up their minds or raise issues of concern.

The last company that I worked for went a step further by setting up a whistle blower policy to allow employees to raise any confidential issue to the top management. The issues varied and may affect their superiors in secrecy matters such as sexual harassment, abuse of authority or even on conflict of interest.

Sharing a Regional Union experience in Asia

This was one of the extreme incidents that happened in a unionized working environment, a company named Suzuki Maruti. Suzuki Maruti located in northern India, is India's largest automaker.

In 2012, the Company was involved in a high profile dispute with the union which resulted in the death of its' General Manager of Human Resource.

Summary of Incident

During the riot between the union members and the management, the General Manager of Human Resource was killed during the attack whereby he was burnt to death whilst a few hundred management members were seriously hurt and hospitalized. Police in Haryana state launched a manhunt for 12 union leaders of Maruti, which majority is owned by Japan's Suzuki Motor Corp., a senior police official said.

Maruti spokesman said that the unrest began after **the workers' union on that fateful Wednesday demanded the reinstatement of a worker who had been suspended for beating a supervisor.** The plant employs 3,200 assembly workers, where about half were permanent and the other half being contract workers.

The police suspected that the 12 union leaders conspired with some workers in the factory and some who had previously been fired to launch a preplanned attack on the factory. The police still continued with the investigation to bring justice to everyone that was affected by the incident.

Lessons learned

There will be cases or moments when union will test the strength of the management in dealing with their demands which at times can be unreasonable. As in the case of foreign workers issue, this is a matter of employment which is clearly a management prerogative by law.

Thus, the company must stay put in such decision and union should not intervene unless the ratio of foreign workers exceeds the limit allowed by the law. There were many cases in the past where the extent of giving in for the sake of good industrial relation, allows the union to encroach into subject matters of management prerogative rights.

This is something that Human Resource personnel need to understand and walking on a tight rope of balancing the act, being nice but keeping the management prerogative intact.

The case of Suzuki Maruti is an extreme example of union retaliation which may or may not happen in this country. Locally we also had cases of union aggression in their show of protests, like a **mock funeral** which took place in 2012 at the peak of a dispute between Kesatuan Kebangsaan Pekerja-Pekerja Bank Semenanjung Malaysia with May bank.

Even though, the mock funeral did not lead to any physical violence to any person, but the action was done with the intention of causing an extreme public embarrassment to the management staff.

Fortunately, until today, actual case of physical violence as what happened at Maruti had not happened in this country. We do pray that such extreme display of protest will never occur in this country.

Managing conflicts and moral values in a unionized environment

We do not want at the end of the day, the management to be caught in a difficult situation of conflicting values and morals. Of course, the intention of such initiative is to improve collaboration with the union, but along the way when the times get tough, such understanding can backfire on the company.

The process of creating a conducive and productive working environment is a mutual effort between the company and the union. The presence of the union has its advantages where it serves as a check and balance on the authority of the management and to avoid any exploitation of employees resulting in their victimization.

There are cases in the past whereby HR personnel were too management oriented ignoring the importance of employees which caused employees to be victimized.

Is a non-unionized working environment always good for the company?

I did come across a multinational company which was not unionized, whereby the company took advantage of employees' ignorance by paying an increment of RM10 for a couple of years. It showed their lack of moral and management ethics on the part of the company, and this is where union intervention may be justified.

In reality, the presence of union serves as a check and balance the way company treats its employees.

Thus, looking from a positive perspective, the company and union, the responsibility of building a harmonious working relationship is supposed to be a mutual responsibility. The union and company should work in a good spirit to build a harmonious working environment for economic success and employment stability in a long run.

We should do our best to avoid the situation of Suzuki Maruti, with due respect to the company, to happen anywhere in this country

Chapter 5

Dismissal

n this chapter I would like to share some important cases which I had encountered and managed during those challenging years of leading the Human Resource function. In reality, dismissal is one of the most difficult tasks in Human Resource function and more problematic if the industry is unionized.

Apart from the personal experience shared, there would be one or two cases shared which occurred within the vicinity of my company.

What is dismissal?
To quote a definition from Wikipedia;

Dismissal (referred to informally as **firing** or **sacking**) is the termination of employment by an employer against the will of the employee.

The law on dismissal

Under the law, **section 13(1)(e) of the IR Act 1967**, dismissal and reinstatement is a management prerogative unless such action is proven to be tainted with a malicious intention or without just cause or excuse.

In **Chartered Bank, Kuching v. Kuching Bank Employees Union**, the Industrial Arbitration Tribunal presided by Sir George Oehlers reiterated the principle governing the Tribunal's approach to the Termination of a workman's services:

Dismissal is a managerial function with the bona fide exercise of which a tribunal will not interfere; where, however, the dismissal is challenged, it is well settled that the tribunal could always intervene if it is shown that there has been want of good faith, victimization, unfair labor practice, a violation of the principles of natural justice or where the decision to dismiss is baseless or perverse.

However, before any employer could punish any workman with a severe disciplinary punishment which include dismissal, **Section 14(1) of the Employment Act, 1955**, it is stated that;

"An employer may, AFTER DUE INQUIRY, dismiss the employee or take other disciplinary action including downgrading and suspension of the employee on grounds of misconduct inconsistent with the fulfillment of the express or implied conditions of service."

A domestic inquiry is an internal hearing held by an employer to ascertain whether an employee is guilty of misconduct. The purpose of a domestic inquiry is to find out the truth of the allegations made against the workman by the employer.

In conducting a domestic inquiry the rules of natural justice must be adhered to. Justice must not only be done but must be seen to be done; the **"twin pillars" of natural justice being "No person shall be condemned unheard" and "No person shall sit in judgment in his own cause or in any in which he is interested".**

Why should the company decide to dismiss an employee?

The company may decide to dismiss an employee on the following grounds;

- Involved in a serious misconduct such as theft, fighting, bribery, sexual harassment, and other similar acts of conduct which is sufficiently serious,
- Repeated attendance problems such as habitual latecomers, absence without leave or exceedingly high MCs without any particular medical problems, and
- Un satisfactory work performance despite being placed on a performance improvement Program,

Even though dismissal is a management prerogative, such action cannot be simply executed based on the whims and fancies of the employer.

The Law and Opinion of the Court

The Supreme Court of India beautifully explains the position of employees' right to employment in the case of **Delhi Transport Corp versus DTC Mazdoor Congress & Others,** where the Court held follows;

"The right to live includes the right to livelihood. The right to livelihood therefore cannot hang on the fancies of individuals in authority. Employment is not a bounty from them nor can its survival be at their mercy. Income is the foundation of many fundamental rights and when work is the sole source of income, the right to work becomes as much fundamental"

The following case studies below are some real incidents which I came across and would share these experiences with the readers.

These were some of the dismissal cases which I would like to recalled upon during my role as Head of the Human Resource department. It was never an easy job to fire an employee because it had a very serious impact to the livelihood of their family.

Case study 17
Dismissing an assistant QA manager
Scenario of the case

This case took place in an electronic manufacturing company in Selangor. I had just joined the company about 8 months when the Assistant Manager was found to have abused his authority in requesting favors from the company's vendors. Being a section head of the QA department, he was accused of requesting favors from vendors on several occasions.

A whistleblower in the organization raised the claims to the company with some evidence, and when HR was alerted, a quick preliminary investigation was conducted. During the investigation, the evidence gathered supported the accusation. Subsequently he was show caused with several charges to which he was unable to give satisfactory answers.

A domestic inquiry was planned to be conducted to comply with legal requirement and industrial practice. As the inquiry date was approaching, this Assistant Manager became very nervous and started calling me in the middle of the night making appeal to drop the charges against him.

As I need to uphold to the principle of justice, integrity and fairness, the inquiry shall proceed as scheduled. This a Company rules and regulation.

Investigation and inquiry

In order that the case was fair both to the company and the Accused, concrete evidences were collected from the vendors and company witnesses. However, a complex situation arose when the key witnesses who were the vendors refused to attend the inquiry on behalf of the company.

They were not willing to testify against the QA manager to safeguard their business interest in the future. They were only willing to provide a written and signed statement to illustrate what had transpired between them and the Assistant QA Manager.

The statement contained allegations of the Accused requesting favors such as money, gifts, special luncheon and etcetera.

I was a bit skeptical with the inquiry preparation due to the reluctance of affected vendors to testify, but decided to proceed with the case. This was based on the principle of the court which decided in many awards 'on the balance of probability'.

Making the verdict

At the same time the essence of the Industrial Relations Act which require decision to be made based on equity, good conscience and the substantial merits of the case without regard to technicalities and legal form(section 30(5).

However the company was shocked when he chose to resign just a few days before the inquiry. To settle the issue amicably, the company accepted his resignation and close the case.

Case commentaries and Review

Even though the company had a strong case against the employee, but the weak point during the build up towards the inquiry was the absence of company vendors who were not willing to testify during the inquiry.

However the company had other strong evidences such as e-mails, hand phone text messages and employee witnesses who were willing to appear in the inquiry which strengthened the case.

I was convinced that if the inquiry continued as expected, on the balance of probability, the employee would be found guilty. In several Court awards, the court will come to a judgment on merits of the case, and not too tied up with the issue of technicalities and legal form which is the spirit of the Industrial Relation Act.

Case study 18
ASSISTANT GENERAL MANAGER RESIGNED AFTER A DEMOTION
Scenario of the case

This company was a subsidiary of the organization that I worked for. The case involved a senior level employee who was an Assistant General Manager of a Production department.

The case was prepared thoroughly by the Human Resource Manager and I was invited to be Chairman of the Inquiry. I was told that the accused had other serious cases in the past which was neglected by the company for unknown reasons. As a result there was already bad blood existing between the company and the Accused.

Investigation and Inquiry

During the inquiry, a few top management employees of the company were called to testify as a company witnesses who included the Plant Director and Senior Sales manager. Since the Accused was a senior level executive in the company, he fully understood the procedures and management system of the company.

There were strong arguments from the Accused who questioned the charges made against him. The HR manager who stood as the company prosecutor became emotional by trying to prevent the Accused from putting his rationale in his defense.

At one point, the Prosecutor of the company tried to prohibit the Accused from questioning the facts presented by the company. As Chairman of the inquiry, I had a torrid time to remind senior members of the company repeatedly about the rights of the Accused to be heard and also to cross-examine the company witnesses during the inquiry.

From the legal aspect, the company is duty bound to allow the Accused to be heard and cross-examined the evident produced in the inquiry. It was quite challenging for me to control the order of the proceedings.

The verdict and punishment

When the inquiry was finally completed, the panel members sat down to decide the verdict and recommend on the case. As chairman of the inquiry, I found the Accused to be guilty on two of the five charges, and thus should not merit a severe punishment such as dismissal.

As the panel member of the inquiry sat down to discuss on the merits of the case, we were visited by the Consultant of the Company who wished to participate and hear the discussion. He was welcomed by the committee. Based on the decision of the inquiry and severity of the allegations which he was found guilty, the panel members decided to recommend for a Serious Warning Letter.

The panel members were puzzled and disgusted when such recommendation was objected by the Company Consultant when he was supposed to be just an observer. He was adamant with his opinion that I had to instruct him to leave the meeting room.

The panel proceeded to put forward the verdict and recommendation for a Serious Warning letter but was not agreed by the HR manager and the company as they had the initial intention to dismiss him.

Company decision

The panel stood firm with the recommendation and we advised the company that a dismissing the Accused would be too harsh a punishment. The company finally agreed to serve a lesser punishment which was a Demotion, to which I still felt a harsh decision. The punishment was not justifiable to the misconducts he had committed.

Since the position of the panel members in the inquiry was only to decide on the verdict to the case and provide recommendation, thus I did not proceed to intervene the decision made by the Company.

As I had expected the Accused resigned from his position and filed the case under Section 20(1) of the Industrial Relation Act as form of **forced resignation.**

Case Analysis and Commentaries

As I was told after the Inquiry was over, it was the company intention to dismiss the employee due to the bad relationship between the Accused and the top management. There were numerous allegations that the Accused had been abusing his authority inside the Plant.

However being the most senior local member of the company, no employee was willing to come forward and bring the case to the top management. The Accused was a person with high level of authority and the employees were afraid of him. When the friction reached an unbearable level, the company picked a case, charged him and called for an Inquiry.

I viewed the inquiry as negative and unjustified, as it contained malicious intention of the company. The Accused, as Chairman of the Annual Dinner was charged for buying low quality watches from the unauthorized vendors to be given as gifts during the Annual Dinner.

As a result there were several complaints made by the employees dissatisfied with quality of the watches. The other charges were also connected to the un satisfactory performance of the Annual Dinner. Legally speaking, even though if the Accused was found to be guilty, the charges put in one basket would not be sufficiently severe for the Accused to be dismissed.

My view on the Punishment of demotion

His job function as Assistant General Manager of production was to oversee the production of quality products, delivery and cost control. These would be the role he should be accountable of, and continuous failure to meet company expectations would make him answerable to the top management.

The earlier cases of the Accused would probably merit heavier punishment should action was taken as when it happened. The organization and HR head had failed to grasp the essence of the **Industrial Relation Act** which stress **on the importance of good conscience, equity and merit of the case.**

Case study 19
Dismissing a union worker for aggressive and violent behavior
Scenario of the case

In this situation, the employee who was also an active union member, was found to have several cases of disciplinary issues which include the followings;

- Many emergency and unpaid leave exceeding the company average,
- Habitual late coming without valid reasons,

- Exceedingly High MCs with a common trend just before holiday and after holiday, and
- Lack of cooperation at the work place

This employee has been working with the company for more than 20 years but was not making any progress in his job grade due to his bad discipline and poor attitude. He was given numerous counseling sessions and a several warning letters in the past reminding him to improve.

However, his poor attendance and attitude continued to worsen and during the last counseling session he had with his superiors, he lost his temper and banged the table before leaving the room. At that moment, his behavior took place in the presence of the Union Worksite Committee Chairman.

Consequently, a Show Cause letter was issued by HR department requiring him to explain his action failing which a severe disciplinary would be taken against him. The Show Cause Letter was delivered to him by his Section Head in the presence of a senior HR executive.

Serious Physical Threat displayed by the accused

However, as the respective Head was approaching him to give the Show Cause Letter, the employee suddenly grabbed a steel chain and started running towards his superior and the HR executive in an aggressive manner.

His superior and the HR executive ran away towards the office for safety and security personnel were immediately called to control the situation.

Actually as he was running towards his Superior, he was stopped by his colleagues and Chairman of the union worksite committee and told him to calm down. There was a brief moment of chaos in the area but it was put under control when the Chief Security and his colleagues came to scene.

Inquiry and Dismissal

The Show Cause letter was not delivered, but was replaced by another Show Cause Letter which contained the earlier charges and additional charges requiring him to explain for the aggression and threatening behavior he displayed against his superior.

The domestic inquiry was conducted and he was found guilty. After weighing the situation deeply from the aspect of the law, merit of the case and its future impact to the working environment, it was only appropriate that the employee is dismissed. I finally dismissed the employee and felt that on the balance of probability, the Industrial Court would uphold the dismissal.

The union understood the scenario of the case and judgment of the inquiry, but did not agree with the punishment which they thought was very harsh. I stood firm with the decision notwithstanding the appeal made by the union.

Union challenging the decision

During one of the union- management monthly meeting, the Vice-Chairman of the Union committee asked me;

"En Rahman, why did the company dismissed the employee when he did not even touch his superior during the commotion that took place, was that fair?".

I said to them, "Look here, this kind of action was very dangerous, especially threatening his superior with serious violence, which if it was not stopped at that point of time, may lead to fatal injuries or even death."

I told them if they were not satisfied with decision, the dismissed employee could still challenge the decision by filing the case to the nearest

Industrial Relation Department under **Section 20(1) for reinstatement. This must be done within 60 days after the dismissal.**

They were a bit stunned with the sincere comment and suggestion that I gave to them. I told them it was never my intention to challenge the union by giving such suggestion, but to inform the avenue they can rely on if they felt, the company had been unfair to the employee.

The case was not filed to the IR department by the dismissed employee or the union.

Case Commentaries and Review

Looking back at the case, I was initially uncertain whether I had a taken a bit of risk in dismissing the employee. True as what was said by the union, there was no physical contact in the incident whatsoever.

But as the case developed towards the inquiry, there was a lot of concerns from the supervisory group and above as they feared if such behaviors were not treated seriously, it would set a precedent to other incidents which might happen in future.

In order to strengthen my decision, I sought the opinion of senior industrial relation practitioners and other experience HR managers within the industry, and they too, had contradicting views of the case.

All the while the union was also watching to see if the Human Resource department was bold enough to dismiss their member if he was found guilty.

When he was finally dismissed, it did send a strong message across the company, especially to union members that the Company would not bow down to any pressure in making a dismissal decision.

On the other hand, it gave the confidence and believes amongst the middle level executive on the credibility of the Human Resource department in executing the rules and regulation of the Company especially in the face of union intervention.

Looking at the Law and Industrial Court Decision

For insubordination, the Industrial Court in the case of Xyratex Sdn Bhd vs Haw Siew Peng award no: 62 of 2012, expressed the importance of highlighting the basic principle when dealing with this kind of misconduct.

Firstly, the court refers to **BR Ghaiye, in Misconduct in Employment, 2nd End.** writes at p. 571 as follows:

> *"When an employee challenges the authority of the superior it amounts to giving formal notice to the officer that the employee will no longer act in the subordinate capacity and will not receive any orders or instructions from the superior officer.*
>
> *Challenging the authority is, therefore, contrary to the basic character of the employer and employee relationship. This will therefore, constitute insubordination."*

Similarly, in **Clarion (M) Sdn. Bhd., Penang & Kesavan Sivalingam Bukit Mertajam** [1987] 1 ILR 288, the Industrial Court held, inter alia, the following:

> *"The Claimant is supposed to be in a subordinate position and if he uses any disrespectful, insolent, impertinent or derogatory language towards his Managing Director, he has committed an act which is inconsistent with his fundamental assumption at which the employer-employee relationship is based.*
>
> *In short, he has committed misconduct for which he can be justifiably dismissed."*

Case study 20
Dismissal for Theft in a Company hostel
Scenario of the Case

This was a case of dismissal which I had conducted against a production worker for stealing in a company hostel. The case happened during my early years as a young HR Manager but it remained in my memory until today. There was a unique reason behind the case which readers will find out later.

This affected employee used to join me in a smoking room during the normal break-time. It wasn't a close relationship but I used to have a casual friendly chat with the smoker group which he normally joined.

However, one day I received a report from the security section informing HR department that this employee was accused by his co-workers for frequently stealing money from them in the hostel. There was no physical evidence to prove the allegation as it was circumstantial in nature.

Investigation and Inquiry

After the report was taken from the complainants, detail investigation was conducted and statements leading to the theft incidents were collected to justify the case.

Finally, when sufficient evidence and statements from the witnesses were gathered, and the Accused failed to provide satisfactory answers to the show cause letter, a domestic inquiry was conducted.

Dismissal

On the balance of probability, he was found guilty and dismissed. A few days later he requested for an appointment with the author who was Head of HR department during that time. There was a moment of concern for me as to the reason behind this meeting; could it be an aggressive reaction to the decision made? Or probably he wanted say some vulgar words to me.

However, to my surprise he came to see me in a friendly manner to say goodbye and gave me a warm handshake saying that he accepted and understood my decision. It was indeed a great relieve and a touching moment in my career and something that I always looks back until today.

Case Commentary

The industrial court had always reminded the employer not to act hastily in dismissing an employee even though the employee was guilty as charged. The severity of punishment for any misconduct should be evaluated on the merit of the case. The fundamental of just cause and excuse should always be adhered to.

It is always a difficult decision to dismiss an employee. When an employee loses a job, he loses a salary which is a fundamental aspect of his livelihood. This will be more difficult when the guilty employee is the sole bread winner of his family.

Therefore, it is absolutely important that in the case of misconduct, dismissal must be treated with absolute care and avoids making such decision hastily. The Industrial Court has always reminded employers not to jump or axe the employee on the slightest issue of discipline.

In the next case study, I would like to recall another incident of unusual situation whereby I had to dismiss an employee who was caught stealing a large quantity of copper wire.

Case study 21
Dismiss for stealing a copper wire
Scenario of the case

As usual, I reached the factory at around 7.45am in the morning. Suddenly I saw the chief security was running towards me to report that one of the employee in Plant 1 was caught stealing few roles of copper wire. He was seen by the security personnel putting the copper coils at the back of his car at the parking area.

However, when the security tried to get hold of him, he managed to escape and disappeared into the morning darkness towards the back of the warehouse. I ordered a full search in the area and he was finally caught shaking nervously under the big water tank.

Inquiry and Dismissal

He was brought to a room, still shaking and looked very frightened. During the investigation, he confessed stealing the copper wires, and I insisted such confession to be in writing. The physical evidence was kept by the Security section and photographed for future reference.

In normal circumstances, the company would consider this case as a serious crime which requires HR personnel to make a police report. However the situation of the employee was so pathetic; looking pale, shivering, tears and begged the company not to send him to the police fearing the worse might happen to him and his family.

It was a sad and difficult situation for me and after a brief discussion with my Managing Director; we only decided to dismiss him without calling for any sort of police intervention.

The purpose was to save him from the possibility of being jailed which might put his family under a more adverse condition.

When he was served the letter of dismissal with no police reports, he thanked the company repeatedly and sought forgiveness for what he had just done.

Looking back at the case: Have I made the right decision?

Until today, I could still remember the case clearly and was not too sure if I had done the right thing from the perspective of good corporate decision. Under normal circumstances, any theft which is connected to company property or assets would be reported to the police department. This is considered as a major misconduct and a crime.

However, at that particular time, sentiment has override a correct corporate judgment and as a result the employee was released with only a dismissal. He was wet, shivering and pale, too frightened even to talk. He had a wife with four children, and with that in mind, I was too sympathetic to bring the case to the police.

I knew it was a right decision from the aspect of humanity but was morally wrong from the perspective of ethical corporate decision.

These were some of the cases that linger in my mind until today when the topic of dismissal was discussed.

Chapter 6

Managing Grievances

What is grievance in a work place?

Simply put, **grievance is defined as a dissatisfaction that disturbs an employee whether expressed or not.**

In one of the **Collective Agreement** that I had concluded, Grievance was defined in one of the Article as;

"As a complaint by the employee concerned which he brings to the attention of his immediate superior and which is subsequently not settled to the satisfaction of the employee."

Why do Grievance occur or what does it signify?

In a work place, grievance is always a symbol malfunctioning or maladjustment. Grievances can arise from the following;

- Victimization,
- Harassment which can either be bullying or sexual,
- Issue of transfer, appraisals, unequal workload,
- Terms and condition such as issue of promotion, salary increment or bonus,
- Discrimination,
- Work conditions such as safety, uniforms, food at cafeteria, etcetera,

- Disciplinary actions,
- Overtime, wages

Employees' Grievances occur almost in all organizations whether they are in a unionized or non-unionized environment. In order to manage the situation properly, most companies establish a procedure to allow employees to file their grievances systematically.

A sample of such procedure is shown in the next page;

Sample of Grievance Process Flow

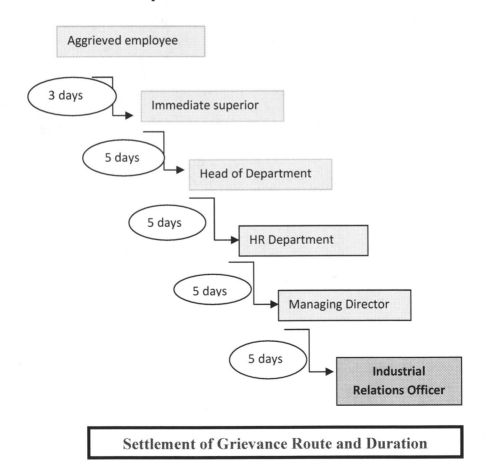

Settlement of Grievance Route and Duration

The process mentioned above is a common flow that can be found in most organizations. The details may differ, but the overall process flow is almost the same.

Requirement of Change in Process Flow

In a situation of conflicting scenario, the process may need to be modified according to necessity, as for example, the employee's grievance is actually against his own immediate superior. Then the first step of filing such grievance shall flow directly to his Head of Department.

Similarly, if such grievance is against the HR department, then the final step in the Company shall be with the Managing Director. If such grievance fails to be resolved to the satisfaction of the employee, then such case will be filed at the nearest **Industrial Relation department as a Trade Dispute under Section 18(1) which states that;**

"Where a trade dispute exists or is apprehended, that dispute, if not resolved, may be reported to the Director General by-

a. *An employer who is a party to the dispute or a trade union of employers representing him in the dispute; or*
b. *A trade union of workmen which is party to the dispute."*

Employers should always realize that employee dissatisfaction is always a potential source of trouble, whether it is expressed or not. Hidden dissatisfaction grows and simmers within the organization that leaving it unresolved may lead it to be completely out of proportion to the original concerns.

Therefore, it is imperative that dissatisfaction be given an outlet. A complaint that has not been submitted in writing is better to be settled early to prevent further escalation.

Definition of Trade Dispute

The term **"trade dispute"** is defined under **Section 2 of the Industrial Relations Act, 1967 and section 2 of the Trade Unions Act 1959 as follows:"**

> *...any dispute between an employer and his workmen who is connected with the employment or non-employment or the terms of employment or the conditions of work of any such workmen."*

Therefore the HR department should ensure that all grievances should be settled amicably within the organization. One of the important principles in handling grievance is speed and should be resolved within the first line of authority.

In managing grievances effectively, the following steps can be adopted by any organization;

a.   **Understand the nature of the grievance – what is the issue of dissatisfaction,**

b.   **Obtain the facts of the grievance,**

c.   **Analyze the facts that cause the dissatisfaction,**

d.   **Find a good and fair solution –agreed by both parties, and**

e.   **Follow up to ensure that the solution is implemented.**

If the grievance fails to be resolved internally, it will lead to a trade dispute which may finally be referred to the Industrial Court for adjudication. In the case of unionized environment, it may trigger other disputes to happen which may creates a negative impact to the work climate of the organization. Trade Dispute solution process is shown in the next page for further understanding.

TRADE DISPUTE RESOLUTION PROCESS

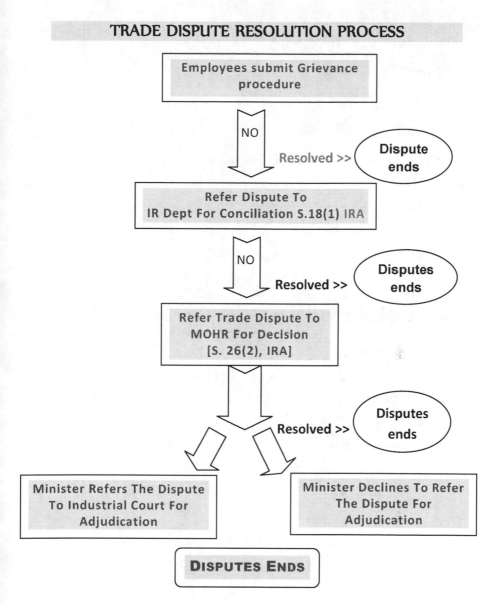

Looking at some of the cases which I had managed in the past, there were several issues of employees' grievances which I would like to share with the readers. They occurred in both environments, union and non-union environment. Let's go through these cases accordingly.

This was the case of a group of employees who were dissatisfied with their superiors for not giving them overtime work over a period of 1 month.

This group employees were dissatisfied with their superior and claimed that they were victimized for not allowing them to do overtime work. Since the grievances were made against their superior, the Grievance Form was submitted directly to the respective Department Head, who after a series of explanation failed to convince these employees.

Grievance submission and case investigation

Therefore such grievances finally came to the HR department for a solution. In order to understand the case properly, a separate meeting with either party was conducted to get the facts correct. Based on the analyzed facts collected, the following facts were discovered; that these employees were excluded from doing overtime due to the following reasons;

They were found to be,

- Habitual latecomers,
- Poor attendance with high MCs especially on Monday and Friday of the week, and
- Shows lack of cooperation in the section.

A meeting with the concern employees was arranged by the IR manager and during the meeting they were told of the reasons for the overtime discrimination. Detail information with regards to their attendance, and MCs record were revealed during the meeting. Apart from this, a report from the superior revealed that they had repeatedly been absent from training sessions conducted.

According to counseling records kept by the section, there were evidences that they have been warned to improve on the situation on several occasions before this.

Justifiable Reasons by Superiors

Therefore, when the superior decided to discriminate them from the overtime work, it was done with the objective of using only the productive and good attitude employees.

The purpose was to appreciate their contribution and at the same time served as a wakeup call for those who were not productive to improve.

Case Remedy

They were made to realize that they were lucky not to be served with stern disciplinary action which was applicable under that situation. However, since this complaint was under a grievance procedure, I had advised the employees to show improvement within the next 1 month, after which if their work situation improved, HR department would ensure that they would be given opportunity to work for Overtime (OT) again.

They understood and agreed with the solution. The Superiors were advised on the solution of the grievances and agreed to proceed with it. A follow up on the issue was conducted and it was completely resolved when after a month, the employees were given OT work again.

Case commentaries

The good thing about the case is, it was resolved in a win-win situation whereby the Company managed to improve the attitude of the employees and at the same time, allowing the employees to have their OT work again.

It sends a strong and positive message to other employees about the importance of attendance and attitude in the work place.

The company had just began to implement the Performance linked Wages system or PLWS in short form. As a result there was a lot of confusion in the early periods of implementation.

However, HR made an extensive effort in ensuring appraisers and appraises understood their role properly. Any non-compliance of implementation could lead to a Trade Dispute because the PLWS is part of the Collective Agreement which was given cognizance by the Industrial Court.

Grievance Submission and Case investigation

As I began to collect the appraisal reports from all divisions, complaints started to reach HR department from some sections of employees who were not happy with their performance appraisal review. An example of such a case came from the Purchasing department.

In this case a senior clerk filed a complaint through the grievance procedure claiming that she was victimized in the appraisal process. Since the grievance was made against her own superiors, thus the complaint was directed to HR department.

The investigation revealed that the evaluation process was not complied according to the PLWS which the company had just implemented. According to the process flow, any changes on the Rating made after the evaluation was signed by Appraiser and Appraisee, required the acknowledgment and acceptance of the Appraisee. This was not applied by the Head of department.

Case Remedy

A meeting was conducted in the presence of the employee, Department Head, section and the author as Head of HR department. She claimed that her Section Head abused his authority by changing the rating that was already given by her immediate supervisor.

During the meeting, I explained on the error made by the Superior which was non-compliance to the PLWS system. **The company was required to comply strictly because the PLWS system was part of the Court award.**

The Law on Non-Compliance

Any non-compliance of the Collective Agreement would allow the union to raise the case under **Section 56(1) of the Industrial relation Act which states;**

"Any complaint that any term of any award or of any collective agreement which has been taken cognizance of by the Court has not been complied with may be lodged with the Court in writing by any trade union or person bound by such award or agreement"

Superiors admitted mistake and apologized.

Based on the investigation conducted by HR personnel such claims were found to be true. The Section Head admitted to the claim and was embarrassed by his action, but gentlemanly apologized for his conducts. The rating was corrected and the case was closed.

The employee was satisfied with the solution given by HR department. In view of the embarrassing situation on the part of Section and Department Head, I took the initiative by praising their effort in rectifying the issue, while at the same time requesting the employee to give her best commitment to the department. I felt that was a soft approach in trying to put back the right image of those superiors.

Commentaries

The cases on the abuse of authority and non-compliance to Company procedure can always be found in any organization. When it happened on the issue of performance evaluation, the impact it created can cause employees' moral and motivation to decline.

The performance evaluation is supposed to drive an organization to be more productive, but when the company failed to implement it ethically, it can backfire on the organization.

Case study 24
Fighting between Local and Foreign workers
Scenario of the case

This is the case of a brief fight that took place during one of the night shift. Even though the incident was brief and minimal physical contact, but when it happened to a senior member of the union, the effect was always a going to be a long feud.

The local employee reported the case immediately to his supervisor during the early morning the next day. The local employee claimed that he was pushed on the chest before retaliating to slap the Nepalese worker on the shoulder.

This incident was brought to the attention of his respective superior and Department Head. However after about 2 weeks, the local employee was not satisfied with the outcome of the solution.

The only action the Superior took was to counsel both of them and released them with a verbal warning. The local employee expected a more serious action should have been taken against the Nepalese worker. He made a complaint to the union worksite committee who in turn forward an official Grievance report to HR department.

The incidents and initial settlement

Investigation revealed that the case started when the Nepalese worker ignored the instruction of the local worker who happened to be on the same job grade as his. The Nepalese worker thought he only took instructions from the Line leader or supervisor.

Since the incident was brief and minimal physical contact, the Section Head decided to close the case by giving counseling sessions to both the employees.

The settlement was not accepted by the local employee and union who claimed that disciplinary action such **as dismissal** should have been taken against the Nepalese worker for starting the fight. This caused a huge uproar within that department claiming the management was unfair to the local employee.

The union insisted that the Nepalese worker should be punished with a serious disciplinary action such as termination.

According to the union, there were cases in the past whereby a local employee was dismissed for similar fights, which was not true and non-existence.

Investigation

However the investigation did not reveal any other worker who witnessed the brief pushing between the 2 workers involved. The local employee submitted a Grievance Form to the HR department insisting that sterner disciplinary action should be taken against the Nepalese worker.

The Grievance form bypassed his superiors because he and the union felt that the superiors had failed to settle the case correctly.

I studied the report and had a lengthy discussion with the management team of that department to understand the case and find the right solution to the grievance. It was a complex scenario in a sense that the union had previously been very upset and making noise on the increase numbers of foreign workers in the company.

It was quite a difficult moment to find solutions that strike a good balance of being fair and at the same time acceptable by the union members. However, it was quite impossible to achieve it knowing that the union members would always wanted something better for their members especially in this situation.

This was a case where the pride of union worksite committee was put to the test and watched closely by their members. It would not be surprise if they called for a picket in case the situation was not settled in their favor.

Union intervention

As I was looking for a win-win solution in this case, I received a call for a meeting with the union worksite committee on this matter. I accepted this unscheduled meeting and was annoyed with the arguments of the committee on this brief fighting incident.

The followings were their arguments with me during this meeting.

Worksite Committee: "En Rahman, we think that the company care and like the Nepalese workers more than the local workers, don't you think so?"

My reply: "why do you say that, any proof to back your statement?"

Worksite Committee: "well, if the local worker fight with another local worker, HR will immediately take stern action, probably a dismissal. Why don't you do the same?"

My reply: "there was not really a physical fight here, just a minor and spontaneous brief pushing. Besides there was no witness who really saw the incident."

The arguments continued aimlessly and finally I had to remind them that any disciplinary action taken is a management prerogative unless they can prove that such decision was tainted with malicious intention.

As usual, the worksite committee threatened that if remedy seemed unfair to them, they will not hesitate to picket outside the factory. Since that was a form of threat, I told them they have the right to do it. I wanted the union to know that, dismissal is a management prerogative provided **under Section 13(3)(e);**

"The dismissal and reinstatement of a workman by an employer"

I knew all along that the union was pushing hard for the Nepalese worker to be dismissed as part of their vendetta towards the foreign workers.

Remedy

Several grievances meetings were conducted with the affected Department Head, affected local employee and HR department. Again, I explained the nature of the incident, and the action that could be taken by the Company.

Even though the first contact was triggered by the Nepalese worker, but the local employee had a contributory factor in the incident by shouting at the top of his voice which was heard by another employee who was about 10 meters away from the location.

Based on this rationale, my proposal was to give the Nepalese worker a Warning Letter with 3 months period of observation.

Face saving solution

As part of the long term solution, they had to be separated from the current location; to transfer the local worker to another section within the same department. However, the union appealed to maintain the local worker in the same section, but instead transfer the Nepalese worker to another section.

This would 'safe face' the union and the affected local worker. I fully agreed with their suggestion. The case was finally closed. It took about a month to settle the issue amicably.

Handling Grievances reported by the executive staffs of the Company

The above mentioned cases were some of the official grievances filed by the employees to the management. As in the case of executive level, their cases were normally dealt directly with respective superiors or reported to the HR department for countermeasure.

As for an example I came across a few cases of executives being badly treated by their superiors, and instead of making an official report they would rather come to the HR department for a solution.

A few examples are illustrated as follows;

Case study 25
A female Executive Harassed by her Section Head
Scenario

This female executive had been suffering from the abuse of her own Section Head who happened to be a female boss. She was previously trying to be patient in the hope that her superior would realize her mistake and improve for the betterment of the relationship.

Instead, this superior continued to harass her subordinates by screaming and shouting at the staffs for any slight mistakes that she happened to see.

The working environment was tense and unfortunately, the Department Head who was a foreigner was not too sure on how to resolve the situation.

Investigation and remedy

Finally, the female executive came to see me and explain the whole scenario and request HR to assist and rectify the situation. I call the Section Head concern and told her about the grievances that were reported to me.

I insisted that she change her approach and use more interpersonal skills in dealing with the staffs and avoid the current approach of screaming or shouting. This kind of management lack leadership skills and attributes of a good manager.

I reminded her to improve and would observe the situation from then on. The Head of Department was informed of the grievances and remedy taken by HR department.

The situation though was not going too well and finally the Section Head chose to resign after continuous reminders from the HR department annoyed her.

Commentaries

Actually the problem lay with the Head of Department who was not able to manage this strong character lady. Being a foreigner, it was difficult for him to understand the culture and values of the local workers, and as a consequence, failed to manage the situation.

Therefore under such situation it is important for HR personnel to act fast and resolve the grievance promptly. Any delay in taking counter measure would have worsened the situation and lead to other matters which could back fire against the management.

Case study 26
A Senior Executive Punching an Assistant Manager
Scenario of the case

In this case, a senior executive was detained for punching his superior while working at the production floor. During the incident, he was quickly manhandled by his co-workers from further aggression and security personnel was requested to send him to a counseling room for further observation and cooling of his tempers.

Investigation

Under the period of observation, he was found to be mentally unsound as he kept mumbling and saying things which could not be understood by other staffs in the room. The situation continued for about an hour, but all the while he was kept in the room under control by security personnel for further observation.

I called the Company in-house doctor for his medical observation and possible treatment. However, the doctor could not get close to him as he would turn physically aggressive. He was left in the room with the security personnel and when he was finally aware and conscious of his surroundings, the company send him back to his family.

Remedy

I met with his Section Manager and Department to understand the case further, and was told that this employee had shown weird behaviors for the last few weeks. According to them, this was probably caused by the work pressure due to the increasing workload during that period of time. He was given a week's leave to rest and recover.

Since the incident was due to mental and emotional instability, as mentioned by Company Doctor, no disciplinary charges were made against him. I considered the case as close.

The assistant manager was not satisfied with the punishment towards the employee.

However, I was caught by surprise a week later when the affected Assistant Manager came to see me to inquire why no disciplinary action was taken against him. Anyway, I sat down with him and explained that the case could not be categorized as a disciplinary issue because the punching was done during the period of mental instability or unconscious state of mind.

He was upset and did not agree with my rationale but had no choice but to accept the decision. I was told later that he was still not satisfied with my decision but did not proceed to the next level, who would be the MD of the Company.

Commentaries

It is a responsibility of the Company and HR department to answer or provide a fair solution to employees' grievances as long as the issue is valid and reasonable. However, as the case described above, the Assistant

Manager should have been wiser to understand that his case was not an ordinary scenario.

Even under civil law, it has been established that no legal action can be taken against a man with unsound mind.

Even though this type of case is not common, but I thought the decision made was correct. Employees need to understand that not all grievances will end to their satisfaction because the remedy depends on the facts of the situation or case.

To resolve a grievance, it is not about who is right or who is wrong, but to find a solution that is right legally and morally.

Case study 27
GRIEVANCES AGAINST THE CAFETERIA MANAGEMENT
Scenario of the Case

The issue of cafeteria management is always a sensitive and delicate matter in any organization especially in a manufacturing environment. To ensure the cafeteria management is properly managed according to the expectation of employees, a cafeteria committee is always there to oversee the needs of the employees.

The purpose of the committee is to ensure that the cafeteria delivers food in good quality, hygienic, reasonable cost and with a variety of menus. The committee shall be accountable to all employees for all these factors mentioned.

However, in one of the organization that I worked for, the cafeteria happened to go through a bad period of food production. There were numerous complaints on the food delivered such as bad taste, poor cleanliness, expensive and related matters.

Grievances

There were several grievances raised in the meeting with the cafeteria owner, unfortunately the quality and service of food continue to deteriorate.

It was fortunate that the vice-chairman of the union worksite committee was also one of the Cafeteria committee members; which otherwise would have cause the scenario to be much more difficult and complicated.

The committee had to bear with the continuous grumbles, complaints and insult from the employees. This went on for quite a long period of time which caused the Chairman of the committee to tender his resignation to the HR department. I appealed to him stay back and be patient about the situation as HR department would come in together with the committee to resolve the issue quickly.

The Remedy

As we worked out on the remedy to improve the situation, there were times when the cafeteria owner threatened to withdraw from the contract. He believed the demands of employees were unbearable and his operation would run into a loss if all demands were to be met.

We proceeded with a slow improvement process and continue to communicate with the employees in making them understand of the continuous effort made by the committee and cafeteria owner.

The remedy was not up to the expectation of the employees, but there was real effort shown by the management to resolve the problems. The most important thing was to show that there was a genuine effort for the organization to resolve the grievances of the employees.

As time passed by, continuous efforts began to show fruits but were still not up to the expectations of the employees. Since the cafeteria matter is a company general issue, it did not contain an element of sentiment to it. Thus, it never develops to become a trade dispute.

Lessons Learned

Grievances may come from all level of employees, and their complexities vary from case to case. As we can see from samples of case studies mentioned, the final authority of finding the solution will rest on the shoulder of HR department and this situation is similar to any other organization.

When the number of grievances increases, it may indicate that the organization is not functioning well, or a sign that the employee-employer relation is deteriorating.

However, as a preventive measure, the Company should analyze the situation consistently by using the right indicators to avoid possible deterioration of the work environment.

Case study 28
Supervisors dissatisfied over Terms and
Condition on Medical Benefits
Scenario of the Case

As the management team sat down satisfied with the outcome of the latest Collective Agreement, suddenly I received a phone call from the one of the production supervisor seeking a short meeting with me. He told me the meeting is short but urgent. I agreed and we met in the afternoon after a tea break.

I was surprised as the meeting was attended in the presence of 2 other supervisors which I was not informed. Anyway, we proceeded with the meeting and I told them to speak up on matters of their concern.

According to the supervisors, they were not happy with the current scenario whereby much of management concern was focused on the union members' demands.

Grievance issue

They felt that the supervisors group was left behind in terms of benefits compared to what the union members are getting. They quoted a few examples such as ATB, medical benefits and OT rate which were better than the supervisory level.

They felt this was unfair and ask me, "En Rahman, don't you think it is better for us to have a union, or should we form a union to help us in this matter."

I was taken aback by such remarks and told them to be patient as we were actually working on a program to review the supervisor benefits. Since this was not a formal meeting, I request the supervisor group to call for an official meeting to hear and explain the issue in a formal discussion.

Remedy

In reality, Human Resource had been looking into this matter for quite some time, but was slowed down during the process of Collective Bargaining. I have made proposals to the top management to improve the medical benefits of the supervisor to make it better than what was offered to the union members during the collective bargaining.

This was to reflect the positioning of the supervisors being the senior group compared to the union members. When the meeting about the supervisors' grievances was reported to Directors of the company, they consensually agreed with my proposal on the medical uplift.

However, it never came across their mind that the supervisors were already thinking of forming a union. This really upset and rattled the top management and insisted that I study the situation closely again and create a communication avenue for the supervisory group to voice any of their concern.

Anyway, I conveyed the positive news to the supervisors and told them to keep focus on the job to ensure that we maintain productivity, quality and cost effectiveness.

Case commentaries

It was a close call for the company if the supervisors really geared up to form a union. It was fortunate that I had agreed with the meeting requested earlier, ignoring it would have been a disaster for the company.

Therefore, an important lesson here is not much on the medical benefits, but to act speedily on employee grievances and allow employees to speak up and be heard.

Case study 29
Union official raising the issue of foreign
workers as a Trade Dispute
Scenario of the case

This was something that was not expected coming from the union. For many years, this organization had been using local employees for more than 2 decades. However, as the national economy improved by leaps and bounds, more foreign direct investors came in to set up their manufacturing Plants in this country.

As a consequence getting local workers to work in the factory became harder to come by. In reality, the demands for getting local workers was so competitive that, the locals could choose to work in one factory today, resign and work in the next factory tomorrow. Or they could even choose not to work.

Rationale of company action

On the other hand, the foreign workers were employed on a fixed term contract, ranging from about 2 years to 5 years. In the event of a sudden economic downturn, this contract can be terminated and they would be send back to the country of origin without any major obstacles.

This allowed companies to have flexibility of manpower movement during difficult times, and to accommodate this, most companies are allocating a small percentage of their manpower to use the foreign workers. This is what normally many companies term it as buffer manpower.

If the Company was to use local workers for this allocation, it would be unfortunate that, during bad times they would be terminated through retrenchment. Very few local workers would accept a temporary status of employment, except for temporary college or varsity graduates who are seeking short term period of employment.

Company Action

Therefore, as the Company proceeded with this concept of employment, the union was looking anxious. We recruited about 150 Nepalese workers, trained and put them in the production floor. They worked hard and within six months were able to run the production as the local workers.

Union Unhappy and Treat the matter as Trade Dispute

The union officials from the Head Quarters was very upset with the strategy of the HR department and wrote a stern letter to the Managing Director and me insisting the Company to stop hiring anymore foreign workers. Their rationale was that, it deprived the locals from getting jobs in the Company.

Few meetings between union and Company were conducted but the management would not back down to such pressure. Going back to basics, the existence of union has nothing to do with the way how company decides to operate, and this is clearly mentioned in the **Collective Agreement,**

Article 5 which says;

The union recognizes the right of the Company to operate and manage its business in all aspects.

The law and opinion of the Court

To elaborate Company's rationale further, in the case of **Hagemeyer Industries S/B v. National Union of Commercial Workers** (Award No: 75 of 1983), the Industrial Court declared:

".... the words 'employment' and 'non-employment' are words of the widest amplitude which have been placed in juxtaposition to make the definition comprehensive enough to include disputes of every nature connected with the employment or the non-employment of workers by their employer.

This definition, in our view, covers every dispute between the employer and his workmen which is <u>connected with the service of the workman, or with the benefits and privileges incidental to that service.</u>"

The company opined that this issue has nothing to do **which is connected with the service of the workman, or with the benefits and privileges incidental to that service."**

Settlement of Conflicts

Staying firm with this issue, we did not budge to the pressure of the union. At the same time, the Company was adamant that the employment of foreign workers was a management prerogative as clearly stated in the

Industrial Relation Act clause 13(3);

No trade union of workmen may include in its proposals for a proposal in relation to any of the following matters;

The employment by an employer of any person that he may appoint in the event of a vacancy arising in the establishment.

However, the union official just refuses to accept any logical arguments from the Company and filed the case to the Industrial Relation department as a Trade Dispute.

Both sides presented the case and finally, when the company rejected their proposal no further invitation for discussion was send to the Company.

A few months down the road, the General Secretary of the union came and told me in a friendly manner, "Rahman, do you know that by taking more foreign workers I will lose the union membership fees. This is our bread and butter. Hope you understand." I nodded with a smile and told him I would do my part to collect the fees from the foreign workers because they also enjoyed all the benefits of the collective agreement.

I was really honest with my intention to collect the membership fees from the foreign workers as they enjoyed whatever benefits were there in the Collective Agreement. Unfortunately, I was not able to collect the union fees due to my retirement.

Commentaries on the Case

As I look back at the cases down the road, the foreign workers was not really an issue, but more as show of protest or power by the union in view of the coming Collective Bargaining.

By raising the issue, it was a kind of early warm up created by the union HQ for their members and to keep the relationship a 'safe' distance from the management.

At the end of the day and when the case was finally closed, the issues just disappeared into thin air. However, it was important that at all time, to maintain a cool head and sustain the relationship.

Chapter 7

Retrenchment and Voluntary Separation Scheme

During the global economic downturn, especially in the late-90s and early years of 2000, many industry operations were badly affected. Supply exceeded demands and as a result many factories ceased operation, while others have to reduce their production hoping for the recovery days to return early.

However, when the situation took a longer period to improve, some companies could not sustain the operating cost and many of them decided to reduce or close the operations. In reducing cost of operation at the initial stage, companies will do this by reducing overtime, freeze on recruitment and selective production shutdown to reduce utility costs.

However, when the business did not recover early as expected, a more serious counter measure will be taken such as retrenchment or voluntary separation scheme. This was a short term countermeasure many companies had to make in order to stay afloat in the business.

The Law and Industrial Court View on Retrenchment

When I had to conduct this painful and bitter exercise in the past I would hold to the salient points of the general principles on retrenchment as laid down by **the Industrial Court in the case of** *Cycle & Carriage Bintang Bhd v Cheah Hian Lim* **[1992] 2 ILR 400 as follows;**

"(i) It is for management to decide on the strength of the staff which it considers necessary for efficiency in its undertaking. When management decides that workman are surplus and that there is therefore a need for retrenchment, an arbitration tribunal will not intervene unless it is shown that the decision was capricious or without reason, or was mala fide, or was actuated by victimization or unfair labor practice.

(ii) It is the right of every employer to reorganize his business in any manner for the purposes of economy or convenience, provided he acts bona fide.

(iii) An employer has the right to determine the volume of this staff consistent with his business and if, by the implementation of a reorganization scheme adopted for reasons of economy and better management, the services of some employees become excess of requirements, the employer is entitled to discharge such excess.

(iv) In the absence of any agreement on the point, an employer is not obliged to find suitable employment for redundant workers.

(v) In effecting retrenchment the employer should comply with the Industrial Law principle of LIFO unless there are sound and valid reasons for departure. Thus, an employer is not entirely denied the freedom to depart from this principle.

(vi) The retrenchment of an employee can be justified if carried out for the profitability, economy or convenience of the employer's business. The services of an employee may well become surplus if there was a reduction, diminution or cessation of the type of work the employee was performing."

Retrenchment

The term "retrenchment" has also been explicitly explained by his **Lordship Datuk Gopal Sri Ram, JCA in William Jacks and Co (M) Bhd vs. S Balasingham** (1997) as follows:

> **"Retrenchment means the discharge of surplus labor or staff by an employer for any reasons whatsoever otherwise than as a punishment inflicted by way of disciplinary action. Whether the retrenchment exercise in a particular case is bona fide or otherwise is a question of fact and degree depending on the peculiar circumstances of the case. It is well settled that the employer is entitled to organize his business in the manner he considers best.**
>
> **So long as the managerial power is exercised bona-fide, the decision is immune from examination even by the Industrial Court. However, the Industrial Court is empowered and indeed duty-bound to investigate the facts and circumstances of the case to determine whether the exercise of power is in fact bona- fide."**

The examples below are some of the cases which I had implemented during my long tenure as Head of Human Resource department.

Case study 30
Retrenchment
Scenario of the Case

When the requirement of the exercise was conveyed to me by the Plant Director through a confidential meeting, I thought it was just a matter of formality. The demands from major customers had been poor, and many workers were just idling in the Plant with very little production to do. Factories within the vicinity had been conducting the exercise, so it was a matter of time when the Company finally decided to do this.

To comply with the process legally, communications on the impending exercise was done with all level of employees to explain and justify the action. Within a few days after communicating the news, a sense of insecurity and worries grasp the factory environment. The atmosphere became negative as employees were very concern with their employment status.

Communicating to Employees

I explained to the Heads of Department on the criteria of selection whereby the company insists the selection would be based on performance within the same job grade or level. We were departing away from the LIFO principle which caught many senior management to puzzle on the viability of its implementation.

I explained the basis of this principle which was not common but acceptable by the Industrial Court. Once the company had decided to adhere to this principle, it cannot mix with the LIFO principle which was Last in First Out.

The objective was to keep good performing employees in the employment and retrench employees with poor performance. From the perspective of the organization, this system will show an appreciation from the company towards good performance employees by providing better job security.

The Law on the Principle of LIFO

The LIFO principle is not an absolute mandatory rule and the employer can depart from the rule when retrenching staff. The departure from the LIFO principle was adopted by our Industrial Court.

In the case of **Supreme Corporation Bhd versus Puan Dorean Daniel a/p Victor Daniel and Ong KhengLiat [Award No: 349 of 1987]**, the court held that:

> *"It must be noted, however, that LIFO is not an absolute rule (it is not a statutory provision) which cannot be departed from by an employer when retrenching staff. That the employer is not denied the freedom to depart from the LIFO principle is made obvious by clause 22 (b) of the code of conduct.*
>
> *"...if, however, in the light of other objective criteria and special circumstances, the employer has sound and valid reasons for the departure from the LIFO procedure, all authorities agree that he should be allowed to do so. This is the guiding principle adopted by this Court".*

The Implementation

In the selection process, it was explained to the heads of department that, employees should be selected on the basis of job redundancies. When a certain number of employees within a similar job grade were required for the selection, such name list should be forwarded to the HR department for detail clarification on the Year-end performance result. This validation by HR department applied to all job grades of affected employees.

When the retrenched employees were finally called to the meeting room for briefing and notification, the atmosphere was filled with disappointment. Even though, the company provided a good termination package for the affected employees, a few of them could not hold their sadness and tears flowed unabated.

Cushioning the Impact

However, I explained to them that HR will do everything to ease their pain by communicating with other companies within the vicinity and also the labor department in assisting them to get back into employment. This was a difficult period for the company as well the employees.

A few of the affected employees challenged the selection criteria, and it was a difficult task trying to convince them. A few of them made complaints to the nearest Labor department claiming unfair labor practice. During meetings with the Industrial Relations department, the selection criteria was explained in detail and samples of affected employees' performance were shown to them.

In the end the case was rejected and was not referred to the Industrial Court.

Case commentary and Reflection

The case was unique in a sense that the Company took the risk by moving away from the normal LIFO principle. To be safe doing this, first of all the Company must prove that the retrenchment is genuine and not as a disguise or blanket or colorable exercise to terminate unwanted employees.

There were few cases that ended up in the Industrial Court where the court made decision in favor of the employees when the Company was not able to justify the retrenchment exercise.

View of the industrial court on retrenchment

Looking back on the case of **East Asiatic Company (M) Bhd. v. Valen Noel Yap [1987]** ILR April 363, the learned Chairman stated as follows:

"For it is the right and privilege of every employer to reorganize his business in any manner he thinks fit for the purpose of economy or even convenience; and if by implementing a reorganizing scheme for genuine reasons of better management and economy the service of some employees become excess of requirements, the employer is entitled to discharge such excess.

> But *this right of the employer is limited by the rule that he must act bona fide and not capriciously or with motives of victimization or unfair labor practice.*
>
> *Nor does this right for instance entitle an employer, under the cover of reorganization, to rid him of employees who have offended him in some way or to promote the interests of some favored employees to the detriment of others.".*

As a responsible organization, I had to find ways to help the affected employees in looking for other employment opportunities. This is not a legally binding requirement but as part of corporate social responsibility in helping out retrenched employees from the adversities.

The Aftermath Effect

In a normal company environment, the negative effect of the retrenchment exercise will take a certain period of time to recover. When I took a walk around the Plant, I could see that morale was low, and few weeks down the road, a few employees walked to me to inquire if there would be another retrenchment exercise coming again.

This traumatic episode left deep scars in the employee minds, and when the global economy recovered many employees chose to leave the company. **They felt that the companies' mantra of 'employees are greatest assets of the company' is empty words without any truth.**

This happened in most organizations that went through the retrenchment exercise. This episode becomes the turning point the way employees are looking at their employment days.

Case Study 31
Personal experience- I was almost Retrenched!!
Scenario of the Case

This was a personal experience which happened to me when I was a young executive coming in to the second year of my working life. I was working with the largest Tin Mining Company during that time.

As a young graduate, the reality of working life was still new to me as life seemed rosy and exciting with all challenges that come in the job. I never knew that something traumatic was just about to happen.

Somewhere towards the end of year 1986, all the branch executives were called back to the office Head Quarter in Kuala Lumpur for a management briefing. None of us were aware what was to come during this briefing.

No Communication on the Retrenchment Exercise

However, as we chatted cheerfully waiting for the briefing from early morning, one of the senior executive whispered to one Mat Ruzlin and me, "Hey guys, don't you know that both of are you in the retrenchment list?"

That really shocked us and no words could express our fright and disappointment. Both of us were speechless for a moment, but pretended to be steady in the face of this unexpected catastrophe. We could do nothing but wait for the moment of truth.

Finally, the General Manager called and invited us to his room and explained the truth about the retrenchment exercise. Genuinely, he was sad and told us that he needed to select one of us for the retrenchment and could not decide. On the basis of LIFO, criteria used by the company, I would be saved as I happened to be 1 day earlier than my close friend Ruzlin.

Making the Selection – throw of a coin?

As we sat silently for a moment together in the room, the General Manager look towards the window, and said, "Can I throw a coin to decide on this? I am sorry but this is too difficult for me." We told him it was ok for him to decide and we would accept whatever decision he made.

Finally, my close friend Ruzlin stepped forward and volunteered to be retrenched as he was confident to get a job within a short period of time. It really caught me by surprise again and felt hopeless by the whole situation. The General Manager sadly agreed and the whole retrenchment episode was completed whereby about 70 employees were affected.

The whole episode was a traumatic experience for me and it took me quite a while to really recuperate from my emotional instability. The guilty feeling of causing a close friend to lose a job caused a temporary depression that took a long time to heal.

Case Commentaries

Until today, about 30 years later, I still had a huge disappointment towards the conduct of Human Resource department during that period of time for not being ethical in the whole the retrenchment exercise. The communication was a breakdown as many affected employees were totally unaware of this exercise.

As a consequence these employees were totally caught unprepared and many of them suffered depression in the months to come. Being a huge organization, the Human Resource department should have been ethical and exercised good corporate governance that complied with the required procedures of retrenchment. This was a clear example bad labor practice.

However, in the early and mid-80s many companies could escape with such conduct, but as more industries moved forward, more employees were aware of their employment rights.

This painful and traumatic lesson in life learned at the young age of my career became my guiding principle in managing this kind of exercise. As the Head of Human Resource several years later, I made a promise that when the need to retrenchment is inevitable, the employees shall endure the pain caused by the poor communication that I underwent.

Voluntary Separation Scheme (VSS)

Voluntary Separation scheme is also another form of termination scheme exercised by companies to reduce manpower on the basis of operation requirement. To understand better how the Court view the subject of VSS, here is an extract of Federal Court statement on this matter as below;

The Law and Opinion of the Court

The Federal Court applied the decision of the Supreme Court of India, *AK Bindal & Anor v Union of India & Anor [2003] 2 LRI 837* where the governing principles for VSS had been succinctly set out; i.e. -

"The Voluntary Retirement Scheme (VRS) which sometimes called Voluntary Separation Scheme (VSS) is introduced by companies and industrial establishments in order to reduce the surplus staff and to bring in financial efficiency...

The whole idea of implementing VRS is to save costs and improve our productivity. The main purpose of paying this amount is to bring about a complete cessation of the relationship between the employer and the employee.

After the amount is paid and the employee ceases to be under the employment of the company or the undertaking, he leaves with all his rights and there is no question of his again agitating for any kind of his past rights, with his erstwhile employer including making any claim with regard to enhancement of pay scale for an earlier period..."

In the recent cases of voluntary separation, companies had improvised the versions by calling it with various names such as Mutual Separation scheme and Voluntary Early Retirement scheme and others. The essence of purpose remains the same that is to reduce the surplus of staff and to improve the operational and cost efficiency.

Importance of Communication before Separation scheme or Downsizing Activities

Communication is a crucial process prior to any process of man power downsizing. Apart from the requirement, the Law and Code of Industrial harmony, failure to conduct communication sessions will lead to employees' unrest and confusion in the workplace.

As for example, when I was conducting the first Voluntary Separation scheme for one company, I took a lot of effort to ensure that the essence of communication is correct and easily understood by the employees.

Several weeks before the implementation, all department heads were informed, and the criteria for selection were clearly spelt out to ensure the right employees were selected. The matter should be kept confidential until announcement was made by the HR department. This is to avoid any misinformation which could be interpreted wrongly and jeopardized the scheme and company operation.

Important Issues to be communicated

In matters like VSS, retrenchment and similar separation scheme, the employees have the legal rights to be informed. This termination scheme affects the employees' livelihood. However, based on my experience, the leakage did happen and before I could convey the news, some employees were aware on the contents of what my communication would be.

Anyway, the HR department is accountable to deliver the message tactfully from the business point of view, the rationale behind the decision and assistance that HR would do to assist the bitter employment separation.

When the message was communicated in a proper manner, the employees will understand but you could still see the sense of worry and disappointment from the face employees.

Without the right information given ahead of such events, things could get very tough for the company. There were many instances whereby employees still made a report of Unfair Dismissal even though they have accepted the separation package.

The period between the late 1990s until the early years of 2000, was rather quite turbulent due to the global economic downturn. Many industries were badly affected and as a result, there were many cases of termination, either forced or voluntary scheme.

It was no exception for me as I had to conduct several employee separation exercises during this period. I was fortunate not to have cases of terminated employees filing the case to the Industrial Court.

I believe this was contributed to the right application of the Industrial Law requirement and proper communication exercises given to the employees prior to the scheme.

Here are real cases which I would like to share with the readers.

As many of us still remembered, there was a serious economic global downturn between the years of late 1990s until the beginning of early 2000s. The situation was so severe that most companies had to conduct the process of downsizing in order to stay afloat in the business. This was one of the most difficult and challenging periods for any HR practitioners.

I had a workforce of about 1800 employees whereby some 300 workforce were made up of foreign workers. In compliance with the Code of Industrial Harmony, the foreign workers were forced to be terminated early and send back to the country of origin.

Communicating the VSS scheme

Yet the business situation requires the company to reduce the workforce further in order to sustain the cost of operation and to sustain business survival of the organization.

Once the VSS scheme was decided by top management, several layers of communication were conducted to all employees. This was the first VSS scheme conducted in the company, and many employees were confused whether they would want participate in the scheme.

When the applications were received and processed, there was an overwhelming application for the scheme from employees which exceeded expectation of the company.

Selection Process

When the actual employees were finally selected, quite a number of employees were rejected. I thought the job was well-done and completed. I was satisfied with the activity conducted because the company has achieved the required number of employees and thus, avoid the possibility of having to conduct a retrenchment.

Something beyond Expectation happened

As I sat down feeling exhausted but satisfied with the outcome of the scheme, a female employee came to see me seeking for a private meeting. During the meeting, I was a little shocked by her strong request and insistence to be included in the VSS scheme. I told her the selection was final and the company would not change the name list anymore.

She was very adamant and insisted that I put her name in the list. She even told me,

"En Rahman, please, I beg you to include my name in the VSS scheme. I am willing to do you a favor for such support".

I had to warn her about such statement and ordered her to leave the meeting room.

She appealed repeatedly through her department Head and it became such a nuisance for the management that she was verbally warned and finally accepted the decision unwillingly.

Looking back, this is one of the astonishing and weird incidents that happened in my role as the head of HR function.

Case Commentary

Looking back in the early years of 1980s, separation scheme used to be a very traumatic experience for any employees as well as the employer. Since I started my career during these years, these activities, VSS or retrenchment was rarely heard and done. When it happened, it caused fright in the heart and minds of employees because jobs were very difficult to get during this period.

In a rare incident, there was a case of employee who committed suicide after being retrenched. However, in the periods that follow many years later, scenarios have changed whereby some employees bravely applied to be considered for the separation scheme.

This was mainly due to the improve employment alternatives and opportunities that continuously grow in the country. The incident of female employee who adamantly requested to be included in the VSS scheme illustrate as an example of this current scenario.

The voluntary separation scheme can take many names such Mutual Separation scheme, Voluntary Early Retirement Scheme and few others, but they are still of the same of species, which is a voluntary termination of employment.

Case Study 33
Voluntary Early Retirement SCHEME (vers)-employee claim forced to resign
Scenario of the case

This was quite unique in the sense that the company was offering an early retirement scheme for employees who above the age of 50 years old.

The objectives were as follows;

- **Giving an opportunity for employees above the age of 50 years old to retire early with a monetary package.**
- **To allow this group of employees who were not medically fit an alternative to leave employment early, and**
- **To allow employer to maintain a good level of productivity by keeping younger and healthy employees especially in the production department.**

Employees above the age of 50 years were invited for a briefing to inform on the scheme and the monetary package offered if they decided to apply and were selected.

The Selection Process and Outcome

After all the processes were completed, only 3 members from the management level applied for the scheme which did not meet the numbers of employees targeted.

Since this is voluntary separation scheme, the process was considered closed. One of the applicants selected was a Warehouse Manager of the company who happened to be amongst those employees who were medically unfit. He used to take lengthy days of medical leaves and his poor attendance had been a matter of concern for the top management. His application was accepted and the scheme was closed a few days later.

Employee wanted to retract VERS application after final selection was made.

About a week before the final date of his employment, the Warehouse Manager appealed to management to retract his VERS application.

His request to withdraw from the scheme was rejected by the top management and proceeded with the termination of the employee. It was clearly stated in the VERS guideline that any application accepted by the company cannot be retracted. He was terminated from the employment accordingly.

However, the employee was not satisfied with the outcome of the scheme, filed a claim for reinstatement under **Section 20(1) of the Industrial Act 1967 claiming that he was forced to resign.**

The Warehouse manager took the package which included the additional package that he was asking for, but proceed to file a claim for reinstatement on the grounds that he was forced to resign.

During the conciliation meeting with the Industrial Relation officer, he claimed that there was a meeting initiated by the Plant director to influence him to accept the Early Voluntary Retirement scheme.

In actuality, such meeting did exist, but with a purpose of clarifying the monetary package wherein the Warehouse Manager bargained for an additional monetary package to be added to the original package that was offered earlier. Since there were only 3 senior employees applied for the EVRS, the company had agreed to the request.

The case was still pending for minister referral at the point of this write up. Since the evidences and documentation for the case was properly kept and file, the company believe and hope that, on the balance of probability, the court might decide in favor of the company.

Case Commentaries

In reality there are many cases of unfair dismissal reported by employees were not genuine, and therefore employers are advised to conduct these kinds of scheme carefully and keeping related documents properly filed for future reference if required.

There were cases that ended up in the Industrial Court whereby employees sued the company for unfair dismissal when in actuality; they were terminated through a voluntary separation scheme or retrenched.

It is quite interesting to elaborate on the subject of forced resignation.

What is Forced Resignation?

The views of the IR Court on the issue of **Forced Resignation** could be understood from the case below.

The law

In the Industrial Court case of **Harpers Trading (M) Sdn. Bhd. Butterworth Kesatuan Kebangsaan Pekerja Pekerja Perdagangan**[1988] 2 ILR 314 (Award No. 251 of 1988) the Court puts it this way:

> **"It is well established principle of industrial law that, if it is proved that an employer offered the employee the alternatives of "resign or be sacked "and, without anything more, the employee resigned, that would constitute dismissal.**
>
> **The principle is said to be one of causation - the causation being the threat of the sack.**
>
> *It is the existence of the threat of being sacked which causes the employee to be willing to resign. But where that willingness is brought about by some other consideration and the actual causation is not so much the sacking but other accepted considerations in the state of mind of the resigning employee, then it has to be said that he resigned voluntarily because it was beneficial to him to do so, that then there has therefore been no dismissal."*

As in the case of the Warehouse manager mentioned at the above, there were no elements of threat, and the scheme was made known to all affected employees. The warehouse manager applied the scheme and signed the document by himself. As a senior management staff, he was definitely not naïve to have signed the important document without understanding the contents of it.

Therefore, in the process of conducting voluntary separation, the company should avoid any forms communications that may contain elements of threat, and to ensure at all times the scheme is purely voluntary.

During the process of doing the voluntary separation, HR or management staffs should try to avoid from having a one to one discussion with the employee to avoid from any possible accusation of forced resignation.

It is also important to note that whenever possible, organization should not jump at the slightest opportunity of doing the termination scheme unless this is unavoidable, and after all other counter measure has been looked into. The activity in most cases will lower morale, confidence, loyalty and employee motivation.

Chapter 8

Collective Bargaining

efore I elaborate on the topic further and the case studies that I will share, let's understand or refresh what is Collective bargaining.

What is Collective Bargaining?

The term **"collective bargaining"** is defined under **Section 2 of the Industrial Relation Act;**

To mean "negotiating with a view to the conclusion of a **collective agreement."**

Whereas a **"collective agreement"** is defined under Section 2 of the Industrial Relations Act, 1967 as follows:

"an agreement in writing concluded between an employer or a trade union of employers on the one hand and a trade union of workmen on the other relating to the terms and conditions of employment and work of workmen or concerning relations between such parties"

These said Articles in the collective bargaining will basically contain items of the followings;

- Scope of employees of covered
- wages, allowances and other monetary benefits
- non-monetary benefits such as medicals, insurances etc,
- hours of work, shifts hours, annual leave
- working conditions

- disciplinary and grievance-procedures and
- statutory provisions

During the period of negotiation, both parties will adopt the principle of agree to disagree, and continue to negotiate until reaching an amicable solution to the process of bargaining. Or otherwise, the negotiation will quickly end up in deadlock.

It is always the intention of both parties to settle the Collective Bargaining amicably, but sad to say this is quite difficult to achieve unless both parties maintain a good common sense and rationality at all times during the negotiation.

Collective bargaining general view between a national union and an individual company

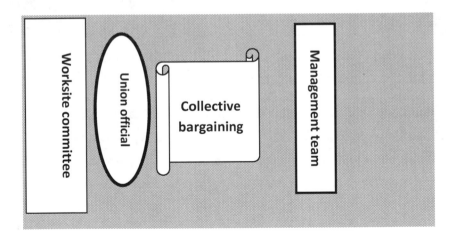

Collective Bargaining

In normal circumstances, the management team will be made up by Head of Human Resource, Finance, Production and one or two other members from HR department in to record the meeting minutes of the negotiation. The union team will be presented by the officer or General Secretary of that Trade Union, and the Worksite committee members. This is the general scenario of collective bargaining in a national union environment.

However, there are cases where the company appointed an external consultant to conduct the negotiation on behalf of the company when they do not have a competent person to do it.

In this chapter I will share my real life experiences on this subject matter which I felt sufficient enough to give an insight to the readers on the general picture of Collective Bargaining. The elaboration of the case on collective bargaining will take a longer explanation because of the complexity of the disputes.

Case study 34
Collective Bargaining
Scenario –Case referred to Industrial Court

It was beginning of the year 2009, when the Company received a new proposal on the 7th Collective Agreement as the existing 6th Collective Agreement was just about to expire at the end of March on that same year. The Union send a proposal at the end of January 2009, and reminded the Company to reply by early march 2009.

As usual, the union initial CA proposals on monetary Articles were always, as we used to described, sky high. As a result, this made it complicated for the company to make a counter proposal that is close enough to the expected level of the union.

In most situations, the initial proposals can be irritating for both parties due to the huge gap that existed between them. However, this scenario can be considered normal as part of the union strategy to achieve as high as they could for all the Articles which they had proposed.

Preparation for the Collective bargaining

The preparation for the counter proposal was a very tedious process, as I had to conduct the followings process;

- Analyze cost impact on all monetary proposals- such as ATB, bonus, salary range, increment and others
- Benchmarking on all proposed Articles- comparison studies with companies and union within the same within the same industry or area
- Review and analyzing trend of court awards for Collective Agreement,
- Study on the effect Customer Price Index, CPI and others

Finally when the counter proposal was given to the union, both parties set to decide on the meeting schedules to proceed with negotiations.

The Negotiation

It was bit of a surprise for the company that, in the first day of negotiation, a president of the MTUC presented himself as leader of the team. He blatantly accused the company of not serious in the negotiation based on the company counter proposal.

The union had proposed a monetary quantum which was very far from what was given in the previous Collective Agreement. To illustrate.

Union Proposal	Counter proposal	Previous CA
ATB -- 18%	3.5	ATB –7.0%
Bonus –4.0 months	1.0	Bonus –1.0months

Note: ATB is salary adjustment across the board.

The objective was to counter the unreasonable initial proposal, something like "if you want to start from an un-reasonable point, the company can also be unreasonable" or "if you want to be difficult, the company can be difficult too". Probably this was the attitude when the negotiation started.

It was quite a bad start for both parties. Anyway, the management, after more than 20 years of negotiating with this union, fully understood the character of the union officials. The important thing to remember in dealing with tough union like this is to remain calm and not to fall into the trap of provocation. So the teams maintained their temperament and remain calm.

To add salt to this negotiation, the employee-employer relation was not good at that period of time. When I came in for the negotiation, I was just about eight months into the job and was still struggling to smoothen relationship that had turn sour during the previous Head of HR department.

As the negotiation became more difficult, tension amongst the union members became unbearable. There were numerous attitude related problems in the workplace but not sufficient enough for a disciplinary to be taken against them.

Communicating with the union members

It was during this period; I decided to call for a briefing on the status of negotiation which was allowed under **section 8A of the IRA which** states;

> *"Nothing in this shall be construed as preventing an employer from conveying to his workmen in such a manner as he may deem appropriate, any information on any matter pertaining to any collective bargaining or trade dispute involving such workmen and the trade union acting for them."*

My action in communicating the status of the collective bargaining received a bad reaction from the union officials as they had tricked their members by giving false information which angered the employees towards the company.

However, the situation did not change the situation very much as the company was taking a very tough stance on the monetary issue. So the tension amongst the union members continued.

Impact of Communication on the Negotiation

However, communication strategy worked and it split the opinion of the union members. As a result, many of the workers insisted the union officials to close the negotiation promptly. Of course, the union leader and worksite committee members were very upset with the initiative taken by the company.

However they did not make any official complaint against the management because of the provision provided in **Section 8(a) of the Industrial Relation Act.**

The negotiation continued again, and it is important for the HR staffs to record all the Articles that were agreed in the meeting because there were occasions when items that were agreed earlier were refuted by the union in the next sessions. Documents for agreed items should be prepared and signed after each negotiation to prevent such occurrence to happen again.

Negotiation Reached a Deadlock

Finally when it was declared a deadlock, the union organized a 1 week picket in front of company premise. They picketed in the morning, half an hour before 8.00am, and half an hour after 5.30pm, which was outside the normal working hours.

It was during this picketing that, the State Assemblyman for Bangi, came to the my office and tried to help in resolving the situation. He requested for a brief meeting with me and my corporate director in the presence of the union worksite committee chairman appealing for the company to agree on the ATB of 6% which was reasonable based on my opinion.

It was unfortunate that the top management did not agree with the 6% ATB proposal. They believed that the ATB should come around 5.0% based on the 2/3 accumulated CPI (Customer Price Index) during the past 3 years period. As a reasonable person I was much disappointed when the Company refused to accept at the proposal.

I repeatedly advised the company in the meeting, "Mr A, that proposal is good enough for the company, as I believe if we go to the Court; there is a possibility that the Court may sympathize with the union and it may ends up at 7 or 8% ATB". The director replied, "Its ok Rahman, if the union refuses to accept our proposal then let's go to Court".

The Case was referred to Industrial Court by the Minister

Looking back at the total scenario of that Collective Bargaining, I felt that apart from the ATB, the company had been fair as we had agreed on many changes which make the overall Collective Agreement proposals better than the previous CA.

Anyway, the union officials kept pushing with their proposals adamantly as part of their strategy to gain more in roads into their unreasonable demands. In actual fact many of the Articles had been settled in favor of the union.

Finally based on mutual agreement between the Company and Union, I wrote a Letter of Joint Referendum to the Director General of Industrial

Relation department to inform that the Collective Bargaining had reached a deadlock.

When the case was finally heard in the court about a year later, the company suffered badly by ending up an ATB of 10% awarded by the Court. That was a huge blow for the company and personally to me, and a big win for the union.

Until today I never put the blame on the union for their victory in the Court decision because they had offered a reasonable proposal during the period of picketing. In fact just hours before the Court made a ruling to proceed with the case, the General Secretary of the union once again approached the Company and asked if both parties could settled the negotiation at 7% ATB, which was rejected by my corporate director.

Why the Court decided in favor of the Union?

The company put in a lot of effort to justify the proposal, but in the opinion of the Court, a huge multinational company that I presented was not in the same league as the other competitors which were found in my benchmark data.

We were consistently making more than RM150 million profits annually during the last 10 years, whilst our competitors or neighbors could not even achieved sales revenue half of what this company had achieved in profits.

Being a company of huge global operation internationally, and with increasing sales revenue yearly, it was difficult to convince the Court that ATB 5.5 was justifiable. According to the Chairman of the Court, making comparison with our competitors or vendors was not fair as their revenue was much smaller and had only managed marginal profits on a year to year basis.

Reluctantly, I agreed with such comments.

Case commentaries

It was a bitter lesson for the company and something to reflect in future collective bargaining.

During the Court hearing, it was difficult to convince and justify to the Court on the 5.0% ATB. Even though the principle of 2/3 CPI of the late Harun J was still being used by many Chairman of the Industrial Court, but the possibility of departing away from that principle is still applicable.

This can also happen in other way round, whereby in cases of companies making a marginal profits or even losses, ATB awarded or concluded could be much lower than 2/3 of the CPI.

Based on this situation, it is important for companies to understand and look at their Collective Bargaining from a bigger perspective. When there is an opportunity to close the collective bargaining amicably on the basis of a win-win situation, I strongly advise that both parties grab the opportunity. The situation would not only save time and money, but build a long lasting and trustful relationship.

Case study 35 – Collective Bargaining
Case Resolved Amicably
Scenario of the Case

This scenario took place in the same company but with an improved environment of employer-employee relation. Employees' grievances were few, union management meetings were peaceful and employees were much focused in the job. The spirit of teamwork between the employees and management were at its best.

When the company and the union sat down for the collective bargaining for the 2nd time after the 7th Collective Agreement, the atmosphere had changed for the better. As usual the union would come up with a 'sky high' proposal, whilst the management countered such proposal with a start at much lower level. Both parties could accept the initial start-up as this was the common strategy for both parties.

However, the positive environment helped for a quick agreement on many of the Articles during the negotiation. Again, when the fundamental Articles of the collective agreement such as ATB, increment and bonus came to the negotiation table, tensions rose again as both parties failed to agree on either proposals.

The Negotiation

During the negotiations the company tried its best to convince the justification made by presenting comparison studies and latest trends of the Court awards. It was simply rejected by the union General Secretary without sufficient counter justification.

This had been their strategy to continuously push up the benefits of the employees without looking at the long term cost impact to the organizations. When I told them on the importance economic sustainability for the organization long term existent, this in turn provides stable employment for all employees, the General Secretary of the union just refused to agree with the point.

Almost Reaching a Deadlock again

Several negotiations later ended up with disagreements and it seemed that the situation will reached a deadlock for the 2nd time again. However the different this time was, the union worksite committee was anxious to close the collective bargaining. They were satisfied with the final proposals given by the company.

Apart from the reasonable ATB proposed by the company there were many other monetary improvements agreed by the company. In actuality during the adjustment of the statutory requirement on the minimum wage gazette by the government, the company went beyond the statutory requirement by also including adjustment to salary above the RM900 which was commended by the union worksite committee and the employees.

At this juncture of the negotiation, the General Secretary of the union was very upset with the stance taken by his committee members.

He was planning to consider the negotiation as a deadlock and refer the case to the Industrial Relation department as a trade dispute, but that was not agreed by his members.

I had told the union that the company has been reasonable with the revised proposals and would not hesitate to go to the Industrial Court if that was what union intended to do.

Union had a Split opinion on the Collective Bargaining

Some of the worksite committee came to see me and expressed their disappointment with regards to the attitude of their Secretary General. Their opinion was supported by the majority of the members.

The Vice-chairman of the worksite committee visited me at the office and said, "En Rahman, please help us to close this negotiation. Our members are not willing to drag the case to the Court again." I told him that was not possible because under the constitution of a Trade Union Act, the General Secretary is the only union authorized representative that can sign the Collective Agreement.

The General Secretary, on the advice of his committee members called for members gathering to evaluate the overall opinion of his members and was stunned when more than 60% of his members had voted to agree with the company proposals.

He was also worried with the rumors that some of his members were planning to form an in-house union to replace the existing national union.

Negotiation Reached an Amicable Settlement

Inevitably, the General Secretary bowed down to the pressure of his members and agreed to close the negotiation. In the process, he lost trust and respect from some of his loyal members.

As for the company, that was a huge relieve to the tough negotiation that took 13 sittings to finally resolved it.

Case commentaries and Lesson Learned

The two scenarios of collective bargaining that I went through were valuable experiences which allow readers to have an insight on the general process and character of the Collective bargaining.

There were several times when the union would say," Rahman, we have to agree to disagree."

However, there were many moments of disagreement that could easily escalated to become a serious conflicts and trade disputes between the parties.

Moving along the process of the negotiation, it is important for the HR personnel to maintain a stable temperament and keeping cool head with all the provocation initiated by the union officials. The company may present a very logical approach in justifying its proposals, but the union officials may strategically, just refuse to accept it in trying to push their demands ahead.

In reality what finally ended the long process of negotiation was the sincerity, rationale and sense of responsibility displayed by both parties.

Collective bargaining —Points of concern

As I look back at the process of Collective bargaining, there are few issues of concern that I felt both parties need to consider.

These are;

- The process of negotiation, and
- The justification of achieving the objectives

As the way it is now, most negotiations are carried out with both parties trying to flex their muscle over the others, and in doing so, make the process harder to reach for settlement.

As a consequence to the egoistic nature of the negotiators, many of the Collective Bargaining landed in Court for an award. I remembered in one of the Collective Bargaining meetings, the union official simply threatens the company by saying, "Rahman, I think the Company is wasting my time, let's go to Court."

During the heat of that session, my reply was the same, "if you think that is better, why not? The Company is ready."

Such stance taken by either party can be damaging from the perspective of good industrial relation. It will lead to a combative nature of relationship between union and employer.

The company and union should always remember the objective of the bargaining, which is clearly define under **Section 2 of the Industrial Relation Act** to <u>**mean negotiating with a view to the conclusion of a collective agreement.**</u>

If every party is aware and has a good sense of purpose, while keeping in mind on the importance work climate stability, the issue of Collective Bargaining shall one day be resolved within the true essence of the Industrial Relation Act.

Secondly, it is imperative that the company as well the union should make a proposals that are justifiable and on par with the market standards. Either party should be able negotiate and justify their proposals with comparative studies, monetary impact and in line with the industry practice. In rare circumstances, a deviation from the above negotiation formula or concept is also allowed if the company is not operating profitably.

9

Conclusion

The objective of these real life cases being recalled and reflected again, is to share with the readers for a better understanding in managing issues related to managing industrial relations. The processes and decisions made were not the only way of managing the problems as it would depend very much on the work environment and the legal aspects required during the period.

The most important thing is to handle these cases legally and fairly. Failure to do this will lead to or trigger a bad industrial relation between employee and employer. In some cases, if such relationship is not remedied early, It may lead to a chain of reactions such as sabotage, low productivity and quality, poor cooperation and consequently affect the company's efficiency and profitability.

In essence, managing industrial relation is not about dismissing or terminating employees but more towards managing and building an amicable and conducive working environment for the benefits of the organization as well as employees.

This is what Section 30(5) emphasizes, to act according to equity, good conscience and the substantial merits of the case without regards to technicalities and legal form.

The case studies described have shown that, some of the conflicts happened due to unethical decision, poor communication and leadership defectiveness. Many of the cases I have encountered, except for the collective bargaining, did not end up with much complication or trade disputes mainly due to fairness and integrity in decisions made.

There are moments when, inevitably the Human Resource department has to make a tough and unpopular decision, but as long such decision is correct legally and morally, and then you have to make that decision. It may complicate matters initially, but as time goes by, employees will gradually realize that such decision taken by the company is correct.

Failure in making the right decision may set a bad precedent which will be difficult to reconcile. Therefore, it is duty bound for the HR department to act according to equity, good conscience and the substantial merits of the case to all level employees, be it a union member or the management staffs.

LIST OF REFFERALS

A. Acts and Collective Agreement Referred

1. DENSO 8th COLLECTIVE AGREEMENT
2. Employment Act 1955
3. Industrial Relation Act 1967

B. Cases and Articles Referred

1. Case of Maruti's Manesar plant GM(HR) burned to death, 91 workers arrested, Bloomberg News 2012
2. Kesatuan Kebangsaan Pekerja –Pekerja Bank Semenanjung Malaysia Malayan Banking Behad Award No: 218 of 2012 [Case No: 1/3-230/10]
3. Standard Chartered bank vs Sarawak bank Employees Union award ward No. 1322 of 2008
4. Dtc Mazdoor Congress And Others vs Union Of India And Others on 14 May, 1986
5. INDUSTRIAL COURT OF MALAYSIA. CASE NO: 26/4-119/11. BETWEEN. MS. HO SIEW PING. AND. Xyratex (M) Sdn Bhd. AWARD NO: 62
6. Clarion (M) Sdn. Bhd., Penang & Kesavan Sivalingam Bukit Mertajam[1987] 1 ILR 288

7. **Hagemeyer Industries S/B v. National Union of Commercial Workers (Award No: 75 of 1983), the Industrial Court**

8. **Cycle & Carriage Bintang Bhd v Cheah Hian Lim [1992] 2 ILR 400**

9. **Lordship Datuk Gopal Sri Ram, JCA in William Jacks and Co (M) Bhd vs. S Balasingham(1997)**

10. **William Jacks & Co. (M) Sdn. Bhd.v. S. Balasingam [1997] 3 CLJ 235**

11. **Supreme Corporation Bhd versus Puan Dorean Daniel a/p Victor Daniel and Ong Kheng Liat [Award No: 349 of 1987],**

12. **East Asiatic Company (M) Bhd. v. Valen Noel Yap [1987] ILR April 363**

13. AK Bindal & Anor v Union of India&. Anor [2003] 2 LRl 837.

INDEX FOR INDUSTRIAL TERMS
USED IN THE BOOK

ABBREVIATION USED IN THE BOOK

ATB   : Adjustment Across the Board
HR   : Human Resource
OT   : Overtime
LIFO   : Last in First Out retrenchment selection process
MC   : Medical Certificates
PLWS   : Performance Linked Wage System
MTUC   : Malaysian Trade Union Congress
IR   : Industrial Relation
TQM   : Total Quality Management

Printed in the United States
By Bookmasters